T0369966

FEARLESS

the new rules

FOR UNLOCKING CREATIVITY, COURAGE, AND SUCCESS

REBECCA **MINKOFF**

HarperCollins
LEADERSHIP

AN IMPRINT OF HarperCollins

TO ALL THE GIRLS WITH NOTHING BUT A DREAM.

it's yours.

NOW GO AND GET IT.

© 2021 Rebecca Minkoff

All rights reserved. No portion of this book may be reproduced, stored in a retrieval system, or transmitted in any form or by any means—electronic, mechanical, photocopy, recording, scanning, or other—except for brief quotations in critical reviews or articles, without the prior written permission of the publisher.

Published by HarperCollins Leadership, an imprint of HarperCollins Focus LLC.

Any internet addresses, phone numbers, or company or product information printed in this book are offered as a resource and are not intended in any way to be or to imply an endorsement by HarperCollins Leadership, nor does HarperCollins Leadership vouch for the existence, content, or services of these sites, phone numbers, companies, or products beyond the life of this book.

Book design by Aubrey Khan, Neuwirth & Associates.

ISBN 978-1-4002-2072-4 (eBook)
ISBN 978-1-4002-5165-0 (TP)

Library of Congress Control Number: 2021934470

Printed in the United States of America
24 25 26 27 28 LBC 5 4 3 2 1

CONTENTS

LETTER TO THE READER

HELLO TO MY paperback reader!

When I first embarked on the journey of writing *Fearless* back in 2019, with the world on the brink of a cataclysmic 2020, I had no inkling of the profound impact the ensuing pandemic would have on all of us. It proved to be a life-altering experience, reshaping our daily lives and serving as a stark reminder of the importance of the timeless principles and strategies for success that I've long championed.

Navigating the turbulent waters of COVID-19 as a business owner, founder, and entrepreneur forced me to revisit the rules and insights that form the backbone of this book, and I am here to report that they served my business and me remarkably well in a very challenging time. Now, as we have emerged from the pandemic, I find myself reinvigorated, filled with newfound purpose, and excited for the future of my company.

While it's been some time since the pandemic's grip loosened, the changes haven't ceased. Since the original edition of

Fearless was published, I've overseen the sale of my company, had my fourth child, and moved eight times. Yet I remain steadfast in my roles. Through this whirlwind of transformation, I've rediscovered the essence of what drove me to write this book in the first place: to embolden you to take the risk, take the chance, and fly without the parachute.

With the release of this paperback edition, my aim remains unchanged: to reignite the flame of inspiration within you. Whether this is your first, second, third, or fourth time diving into these pages, I want to give you a dose of what it took to make my company a success and pass on lessons of grit, resilience, and fearlessness for you to retain after reading this book. The principles outlined within these chapters aren't just about empty motivational slogans—they're the gritty, unvarnished truths that have guided me to success, happiness, and boundless creativity time and time again.

As you embark on your own journey through the twenty-one rules laid out in *Fearless*—and as my gift to you a bonus chapter (22!)—my hope is that you'll find them as transformative and empowering as I have. Apply them to your life one by one, or all at once, and witness the profound impact they have on your path to success.

Thank you for choosing to come with me, for being part of this incredible community of loyal followers, fans, and customers. Your support means the world.

With gratitude and much love,

xx *RM*

Rebecca

INTRODUCTION

I NEVER SET OUT to be a rule breaker. It's just that the old rules weren't really working for me, so I had to go out and make my own.

Had I followed the old rules, I assure you there would be a 0 percent chance that you would be reading this book right now. If I had taken the safe route and always done as I was told, when I was told, where I was told, I'm pretty sure I would be answering the phones at my father's office in Florida. Not that there is anything wrong with working for my dad, or answering phones; it just wasn't what I was meant to do. I find it much more fun being a fashion designer and serial entrepreneur.

Two decades ago, I designed a shirt—we soon started calling it The Shirt—that mixed ideas from my favorite tourist-destination T-shirts to create an ode to my favorite city: New York City. An actress wore it on *The Tonight Show*, and the next day people everywhere knew my name. It's the kind of story that, looking in from the outside, makes it seem like it just takes a little bit of luck to become an overnight success. In actuality, I had been living in New York, in a tiny walk-up shoebox that was advertised as an apartment, and working long hours for little more than minimum wage in the fashion industry for two years before this moment. There was nothing overnight about it. It wasn't until four years later that I designed my first handbag, the Morning After Bag, a.k.a. the MAB, and my business actually took off. Let's also be clear about "taking off": I had inbound interest. What I didn't have was a huge staff or a bottomless bank account. Figuring out how to fan that flame on my own was all-consuming.

Today, after years and years of early mornings, late nights, and good old-fashioned hard work, there is Rebecca Minkoff, the brand. As the founder, I get to be the chief creative officer of a global company with a range of apparel, handbags, footwear, jewelry, and accessories that are all available online and through over nine hundred retailers around the world. I also host a podcast called *Superwomen* and created the business network Female Founder Collective. Oh, and I live with my husband and three kids in Brooklyn. Out of breath yet? I am.

Along the way, I realized that often the world around me dictated what should be done, as well as where, how, and why I should do it. I tried to follow the rules, to go about getting things done in the conventional ways, and to fall in step with the pack. It just never worked out the way I thought it would or should. Eventually, I stopped seeing the point in doing things the same way that they have always been done just for the sake of playing it safe. So then I would do it my way, piecing things together as I went. The majority of the time, even when it would have been much easier just to go with the flow, I've found myself doing my own thing. I've made my own rules and been successful in the process. If that's rebellion, then call me a rebel. It's not about the labels for me. My goal has always been to get shit done.

Throughout these years of hard work and discovery, I learned some things along the way. I didn't learn *all* of my rules for unlocking creativity, courage, and success the hard way—just most of them. (And some of those I had to learn over and over again until life was convinced I had finally gotten the memo.) These rules are a collection of the life lessons that have helped me shape the way I approach situations; they're not an exact decree of how to handle them. They are the small truths that have helped push me forward even when things have felt scary or impossible, even when it felt like game over.

So where did all these lessons and new rules get me? Were the hard work, the hellish nights, and the sacrifice worth it? Give me a hell yeah. Or an amen.

In the last fifteen years, my company achieved over $100 million in sales, has been distributed through over nine hundred points of sale, and has been featured by *Glamour*, *Marie Claire*, *Vogue*, *Fast Company*, *Time*, and a long list of other national and international media outlets. My clothing and accessories have been spotted on the most stylish women (some famous, some that should be) around the world and across social media. As a company, we've been heralded as a place where true innovation happens, and we've been lauded as an example for others across the fashion and technology industries to follow. When I stop to compare the young woman I once was—with two old suitcases and nowhere to live—to the woman I am today—an award-winning, globally recognized designer with a successful brand known the world over—yes, I can honestly say it's been worth it.

I'm not bragging when I tell you this. I want you to know that if I can do it, you can too.

But before we go on, let me be clear: if you hate the idea that shifting your thinking and reaching your goals will take work and dedication, then you may as well stop reading this book now and start using it as a doorstop. (Unless you are reading a digital version. Don't use your Kindle as a doorstop. It isn't heavy enough.)

I totally get it: we're living in a time of immediate gratification, so hearing that overnight success is a myth is a real drag. Social media shows us what it's supposed to look like when we wake up in a perfect house, eat a perfect breakfast, put on a perfect outfit, and broadcast all of the amazing things that seem to happen every day. Why can't it be as easy as it looks? Why can't it happen as fast as it seems like it should? Because creating a dynamic life isn't simple, and building lasting success doesn't happen fast.

There's work behind every one of those perfect pictures: a dozen comforter-and-pillow combinations (and a touch of concealer) for that #wokeuplikethis shot, four versions of the breakfast bowl poured down the drain because the acai turned the bee pollen green. For every celebration, there's at least one far-from-pretty outtake that never makes it on the feed. The truth is just out of frame. Everything takes work, especially success. Even the things that look effortless.

The experiences that have made me who I am today and the lessons that I've learned from my twenty years as a scrappy, determined workhorse trying to make it in fashion are in this book. All of the important ones, anyway. My hope is that these ideas will help you to feel more empowered and courageous, allow you to feel more creative when it comes to thinking and problem-solving, and inspire you to find out what success really means to you, not everybody else.

So here are my new rules. Take them or break them; it's up to you. The beginning is now.

Rule #1

SIGN YOUR OWN PERMISSION SLIP

give yourself
permission to
stop asking
for permission

The first dress I ever designed for myself was for my bat mitzvah. A few years before, I had seen a polka-dot dress in a store window and became obsessed. It was just a simple A-line shift dress, but to me it was the coolest dress I had ever seen in my life. Even though I couldn't touch it, in my mind, I knew it was made with the softest cotton I'd ever felt. The sleeves had just enough pouf to be stylish without feeling kooky or too kiddie. I knew it would land right above my knee if I ever had a chance to try it on. Like most kids, I begged my mom to buy it for me. And, unlike most moms, my mother said, "I'm not going to buy this for you, but I'll buy you fabric and you can make it." That was a real light bulb moment for me. I had been crafting and making cutesy, fun things like aprons and pot holders, and I'd been using puffy paint and sewing patches on my jean jackets, but this felt like a revelation. If I designed something fashionable, did that make me a fashion designer? That sounded really cool.

Asking my mom for things and having her turn me down was pretty much par for the course. But the truth is, she just wanted to teach me how to figure things out for myself. She didn't buy me that dress, but she guided me as we made one—and I thought it was even cooler than the one I had seen. Now, I was twelve, and between the idea of becoming a "woman" for my bat mitzvah and having a size AA training "bra" (think: stretchy cropped undershirt), I very much felt like I needed a dress that would highlight and showcase my chest. (Why, you ask, was my focus on my chest instead of on my Torah portion? Tweens aren't exactly known for their impeccable priorities.) This became my first design challenge. I decided on an empire waist with a square neck and a little princess puff sleeve, and I made it out of white matte silk. I made it just above my knees so that you could see my gams when I sat on the *bima* (that's Hebrew for the stage). My mom wouldn't buy me new shoes for just one night, so a family friend lent me her cream-colored pumps that matched the color of my dress exactly. I wore them with pride even though they were a half size too small. (But I did spend most of the time up on the *bima* worried that I was losing circulation in my feet.)

Thanks to my mom shutting me down, I got way more out of the experience than just an amazing (go with me here) dress. Sewing something that I could wear gave me confidence. The idea of turning nothing but a piece of fabric and some thread into something I would actually wear out in the world seemed like magic to me. I would do as many chores around the house as I possibly could in order to earn money and then spend it all on fabric. When I was out of fabric and out of cash, I would go through my closet and find pieces that I was tired of, take them apart, and make something new to wear. Taking the clothes apart allowed me to see how the clothes were made, and then I could replicate the look if I wanted to.

WHEN LIFE THROWS YOU LEMONS — OR FLORIDA ORANGES

I was born in San Diego in the eighties. It was absolutely as fun as it sounds.

My early life in California was a truly idyllic time period. The weather was always perfect, my two older brothers and I could go outside and play at night unsupervised, and I spent weekends boogie-boarding or selling jewelry at the flea market while my mom sold her Amway products. My dad had just finished his residency in pediatric medicine and had opened his own practice. He worked a lot, but when he was home, he was all ours. We were not wealthy by any means, but my life felt rich. My elementary school self already knew that I was going to marry Steve and that Sarah, Caren, Rachel, and Tami would be my bridesmaids. I was going to wear a ruffled one-shouldered white organza minidress, and my bridesmaids would each wear their own unique look that reflected their personality, but it had to be coral pink, obviously, because the wedding would be on the beach.

Cue the mic drop.

Shortly after I turned eight, my parents told us we would be moving to Florida, where my dad would be taking a short sabbatical. All I knew about Florida was that there were alligators in the swimming pools. I remember coming home and my parents breaking the news to my two older brothers, Uri and Max, and me. They presented it like it was an adventure, and I was completely not on board. As I sat there panicking about losing my friends, my dad sold us on the move with big talk of a house on the ocean, building sand castles in the front yard, and promises that he would have tons of time off to play with us. So we packed up. Everything I owned, which primarily consisted of Barbies, Barbie clothes, Barbie gear, and a Barbie Dream House, was in boxes and ready to be loaded onto the moving truck. On my last day of third grade, my classmates gave me a memory book full of photos and drawings from my elementary school friends. I'd never held anything as tightly or cried as hard as I did that day.

THE BIG ADVENTURE

We piled into our sedan, hitched up the U-Haul, and drove across the country in true Griswold-family fashion. It was the absolute worst. The whole time, I had to sit in the middle seat, squished between Uri and Max, because I could never yell out "Not it!" fast enough. At any given point during our drive, I was either being used as a pillow or an armrest. There were a lot of tears: like when my personal stash of mini candies fell out of the trunk into the muddy parking lot, or when we pulled into New Orleans and I felt completely haunted while semi-lost from my family, or when my dad fell asleep at the wheel in the middle of the night and we did not one but two 360s across the freeway. It was the longest, crummiest week of my eight-year-old life. But at least we were moving somewhere awesome, right?

Wrong.

The night that we arrived in Florida, we were tired, it was hot, and I was sure that when my dad pulled into the dilapidated, half-rotted apartment complex, he had made a wrong turn. It was just like *The Karate Kid*, but I wasn't Danny La-Russo and there was no Mr. Miyagi waiting to give me a shiny yellow convertible. I remember piping up to say, "Dad, you made a wrong turn. We are not at the beach." He replied, "Oh no, honey. This is correct. We decided this would be much better." We went upstairs to a two-bedroom, one-bathroom apartment that was roughly the size of our living room back in San Diego. The place smelled. Mold was everywhere. My heart sank. Even our two dogs seemed grossed out. This was not part of my plan.

I woke up the next morning before everyone else. I threw on my Chucks and ran out the door, determined to find the mythical sand and magical beach that Dad had promised. I knew it was all wrong the moment I stepped outside and didn't feel the tangy taste of saltwater surrounding me. Lo and behold, all I saw was dirt. It could have passed as sand-colored dirt, but it was definitely dirt. That's what was at the bottom of the stairs. That's what I was supposed to turn into castles? And where was the water? How was I going to fill the moats of my princess castle without the ocean nearby? I had promised Barbie a beach day, and she was going to be pissed. Even more than me.

I quickly ran back up the steps, found my father, and demanded, "Dad! Where is the beach? And the sand?" His reply: "That's sand! Right at the bottom of the stairs!" The first few months went like this for everything we did. When I looked for the Floridian version of the fun downtown we had grown up with back in San Diego, where kids could innocently loiter, he told me it was out there somewhere and we would find it. When I looked for the group of really nice, super-friendly girls my age who were destined to be my new best friends, he told me I was sure to meet them soon. When I wanted to boogie-board, there wasn't even a wave. And what I did find wasn't helping the situation: I missed the soft green grass of California, but all I had to look at was dry, hard, spiky patches of Florida turf. I had always liked being connected to our Jewish community back home, but the jerky tweens at the temple in our new town made fun of me for my buck teeth and frizzy hair. I was constantly disappointed, and I missed my old life deeply.

The only saving grace was that it was temporary. At least that's what I thought. Since the plans were up in the air, my parents rented furniture instead of buying it or moving our old stuff out from California. I marked the day our first furniture-rental contract was up on the family calendar. When the big day finally arrived, I ran to tell my dad: "Hey, Dad! We have to return the furniture! Does that mean we can go home now?" He turned to me and very casually said, "We're not going home. We're going to stay." My parents had found a small piece of land that was going for a good price and had decided to save up to build a house of our own. I knew at that moment that my fate was sealed. I was stuck there for good. (And, Florida, if you're reading this, please don't take offense. I've grown to love you, and you know it.)

Even now it stings. I say this fully aware, as an adult human, that I was very lucky to have a roof over my head, to have a loving family, and to always have food to eat, but San Diego was all I knew. When everything you have ever known as a child is ripped from your life, it has a huge impact, whatever your circumstances may be. This was like a bad after-school special, but it was my real life—though it wasn't the last disappointment I would face, so technically it was training.

So why was Florida so bad? Let's unpack this:

- It was hot—the kind of hot where you just are never not sweating. All the time. I couldn't even walk from my mother's car to the front of the school without my sweat staining my shirt.

- I had very few friends. I thought I had made some, but Chrissy turned out to be a traitor in junior high when she up and decided I was too nerdy and awkward to be seen with in public. I wound up getting bullied left and right and dreaded every morning that I had to get up and go to school.
- My older brothers turned into teenagers and left me behind. While they were suddenly doing all the normal, eighties-movie high school stuff, I was stuck at home, playing with my dolls, and waiting for my hot-glue gun to warm up.
- On top of everything, we were the only Jewish people for miles and miles, which made us the talk of the town.

All of this is to say that I found myself flying solo. A lot. Depending on my mood, it either felt as if I had all the me-time in the world or as if I had been forced into isolation. The upside of it all is that it gave me the space to discover creativity. Crafting saved my life. (Does that sound dramatic? I hope so. I really want it to.) I was a mini Martha Stewart always ready with my Mod Podge and handful of puffy pom-poms. My mom had given me an old sewing kit and showed me the basics. It wasn't long before I was making scrunchies for myself and avant-garde outfits for my dolls.

Out of everyone at school, my favorite person was Miss Laurie, the art teacher. She had moved to Florida from New York City, where she had been a print designer. Now she handed out construction paper and was on scissor patrol for a bunch of kids. Miss Laurie was kind and soft-spoken, and she used validation and encouragement to keep you going. She could always find something in whatever mess we kids were working on to compliment. After school, she taught art classes out of her home. For twenty dollars an hour (her rate was actually thirty dollars an hour, but my mom insisted that I negotiate her price down), she would teach me whatever I wanted to learn. Over five years, we drew, painted, illustrated, sketched, knit, and crocheted, and, most importantly, she taught me to follow a pattern and use a sewing machine. Thanks to her (and the extreme nothingness of Florida at the time), I found my love of fashion, art, and design.

DON'T ASK; DO

From then on, I was hooked on doing things for myself. When I decided I wanted to go to the performing arts high school that was forty minutes away, I mapped out the bus route and got myself there and back. How much I earned doing chores around the house or scooping ice cream at the local ice cream shop, where I worked after school and on weekends, was how much I could spend. The responsibility was on me. At a certain point, making things, doing things, and figuring things out on my own became second nature to me.

With my love for all things fashion, it wasn't a surprise that, when I was eighteen, I decided I wanted to move to New York to work in fashion. My mom said, "If you want to go, go." That was all I needed. She wasn't giving me permission. She wasn't saying yes or no. She was putting the responsibility exactly where it belonged: on me. A few years ago, I finally asked my mom why she didn't help us kids out more. She explained that when she turned eighteen and moved out of her parents' house, she didn't know how to do anything. She felt like too much had been done for her, so she had trouble knowing how to live on her own. As a parent, I've learned that is the greatest gift we can give our kids—just a push in the right direction. (Thanks, Mom. Love ya.)

I didn't have a plan. I wasn't sure how I was going to make it happen. But I knew I was going to figure it out.

SIGN YOUR OWN PERMISSION SLIP

We spend so much of our lives waiting for permission. As little kids, we ask our parents if we can do just about everything. We ask for snacks, for toys, or if it's okay to go out and play. We even ask our teachers if it's okay to go to the bathroom. By the time we're adults, we've been conditioned to look outside ourselves for someone to give us permission to do even the little things.

But do we really have to?

No.

Really, the only person you need permission from is yourself. Not your parents. Not your friends. Not society. When we ask someone else to validate our choice before we make it, it puts the responsibility on that person. Suddenly, it's their problem if something goes wrong. Getting outside validation protects us from feeling like it's all on us if we screw up. And on some level, we're all afraid of screwing up.

But here's the thing: if we get permission to do something, or validation before we do something, we aren't off the hook. We still have to deal with the fallout. We're still the face of the mistake. Often, the only person who actually cares, or even knows, that someone gave you permission is yourself, so if you want to do something, do it. If you want to wear something, wear it. If you want to try something new, by all means, go for it. Whatever happens next is yours to own. It's all you.

Rule #2

GO FOR PURPOSE OVER PAYOUT

happiness is
not a time card

As much as I complain about our move to Florida, I'm glad it happened. It only took me twenty-four years to realize it.

Had we stayed in San Diego, my life would be completely different right now. My tween years would have definitely been easier, but maybe I would have been out having too much fun with my friends to ever pick up a sewing needle. Maybe I would have gotten married in a minidress on the beach (instead of in a minidress in Tuscany). Maybe I would have stuck with dance instead of falling in love with design.

When it came time for high school, I wanted to go to the performing arts school that was inconveniently located forty minutes from our home. I wanted to take art and design classes, but I didn't have a portfolio like all of the other applicants to the arts program. I did have years of ballet classes under my belt, and I pieced together some choreography for an audition. By some miracle, this five-foot-nine, size D bra–wearing ballerina was accepted into the dance program. But not fitting the typical description of a willowy, classical ballet type, I never made it onto the performer list. It really brought me down, in the Tori Amos / Sarah McLachlan / Cranberries / moody-teenager kind of way. After a few months of watching the other dancers from the wings and feeling sorry for myself, I made my way to the costume department. It became my happy place.

Being backstage turned out to be the creative outlet that I didn't know I truly needed. I got to spend four hours a day making whatever I wanted, and I was able to completely focus on what I loved doing. I had total creative control. Mrs. Terry, the costume studio director, was used to kids avoiding her. It seemed like everyone was more interested in being in the spotlight instead of behind the scenes. Not me. I was as eager as they come, and she was elated to finally have someone who was as excited about putting together theatrical getups as she was. Mrs. Terry took me under her wing and taught me everything she knew: draping, pattern making, character design, how to bring sketches to life, and more. Nothing was more satisfying than seeing an actress wear a costume on the stage that I had designed. I knew that I had found my calling.

NEW YORK OR BUST

Once I started taking design seriously, I began to believe there was a future in it for me. But it was clear that I would need a change in scenery. When I dreamed about working in the fashion industry, I dreamed about being in the center of it all—and that was not Florida.

Forget about chain stores that sold pocket tees and khaki pants. I wanted to be able to walk into boutiques where the buyers knew where fashion was headed and had their own style and point of view. I wanted to be around designers and other people who were not only passionate about clothing and accessories and what they wore every day, but who also took things a step further and dreamed of ways to build on those designs. I wanted to be inspired. New York had all the labels, stores, magazines, editors, suppliers, and factories. It was the home of Fashion Week in the United States. It was where Calvin Klein, Michael Kors, Kate Spade, and Vera Wang all got their starts. (Paris would have been nice, too, but I didn't speak French and wasn't feeling brave enough to tackle Europe on my own.) My mind was made up. I had to get to New York. There really was no other option.

For as long as I can remember, as a Hanukkah gift, I got to choose a subscription to one of my favorite fashion magazines. It was the highlight of every year. Whenever an issue would arrive, my older brother Uri would somehow always steal it, spend a week reading it, and then hand it over to me begrudgingly. I would eat those magazines up. They taught me about New York and showed me that it was where I had to be. I was a big fan of *W* magazine, *Vogue*, *Elle*, *Harper's Bazaar*, and *Cosmo* (I mean, how racy!). In those magazines, I was seeing the future of fashion. I was inspired by the models who were decked out in clothes that looked nothing like the Abercrombie plaids or the black straight-edge slogan tees my classmates were wearing.

As I got closer to high school graduation and saw all my peers applying to college, I knew in my heart that college was not my path. And my parents, with their hippie values, didn't really care if I went. They just needed me to do *something*, but whatever it was going to be was up to me.

I started to dig around and see if someone might know someone who might know someone who might know a designer in New York City. I didn't have to look too far: my brother came home from a party one night and said a friend of a friend of a friend worked for a designer in NYC. And he had gotten the phone number! My heart practically leaped out of my chest, and I smiled so hard my lips cracked.

I worked up my courage to make the call, and, within a few days, I was dialing in to a call with the designer's assistant. It lasted all of thirty seconds (and that's including the time I was on hold), but I could feel the weight and importance of what was about to happen. It went like this:

ASSISTANT: Can you work Monday through Friday?

ME: Yes.

ASSISTANT: And you're fine with minimum wage?

ME: Yes.

ASSISTANT: Okay. Call me when you get here.

I had to pinch myself. I was disproportionately overjoyed to be hired for a job I knew nothing about and for which I would be getting paid barely anything. But it didn't matter.

To this day, that call remains one of the most important phone calls of my life. I knew practically nothing about this designer. I didn't know his work. I didn't know his collection. I didn't even know if I liked the collection. And I didn't care. All I cared about was that I had a paid internship with a designer and a way forward. I was determined to be the best intern they had ever had and to show them that I had what it took to earn my way into the company. Having this gig in place allowed me to make the jump. So, the fall after high school, when most of my friends were off to their freshman year of college, I left home to move to New York City.

When I told my parents, they were glad to hear I had a plan. In a shocking turn of events, they bought me a one-way ticket to Long Island's MacArthur Airport (it wasn't New York City, but it was close enough and much cheaper than flying into JFK).

The flight seemed to last forever. I couldn't wait to get to New York and start my life. With two suitcases and a backpack full of tiny stolen bags of airplane peanuts and pretzels in tow, I landed on Long Island, spent the night at my aunt's house, and then took the train into Manhattan. Without anywhere to live. I had a friend at Fordham who said I could crash on his dorm room couch until I found a place. Getting an apartment, with how much I moved around as a kid, didn't seem like a big deal, but I had no clue that renting in NYC was a little different than renting in Florida.

Two things became clear really fast:

1. My packing job sucked. I needed a coat. And socks. And maybe some boots? I was used to Florida weather and thought winter just meant putting on a long-sleeve shirt instead of a tank top.
2. Rent was really, really expensive: per month, even the cheapest studio I could find—the toilet was literally next to the stove—was double what I was making as an intern. If I was going to stay in New York, I was going to have to get creative. And find some roommates.

The only family I had in Manhattan was my cousin. She was a single mom, living uptown with her young daughter. She didn't have an extra bedroom, but she did have a playroom. It was covered in stuffed animals and alphabet blocks, but it was big enough for a blow-up mattress. I asked her if I could sleep there, and, in exchange, I would babysit for her twice a week. She agreed, on one condition: I had to pack up all of my belongings every morning, so that her kid could still use the space. For eight months, I woke up every day, deflated that mattress (I can still hear the *rrrrrr-rrrrrr-rrrrrrrrr* sound of that electric pump), and erased any trace of evidence that an eighteen-year-old had been there.

Eventually, I saved up enough to rent my own room—not my own place, but my own room. I had looked through the classified section in the *New York Times* every day until I finally found something I could afford. It was a room on the *upper* Upper East Side: my roommates were a sixty-year-old woman, Carol, and her ninety-year-old mother, Margie. Seeing as I didn't have a stick of furniture to my name, I was lucky that the room was furnished. The décor was that sort of contemporary nineties look that could only be achieved by using synthetic materials like high-gloss plastic and discounted linoleum.

Every morning, Carol would inspect my room to make sure that I had made my bed to her exact standards and that I wasn't hiding anything nefarious in there, like a boy. It was what I imagined going to bad-kid boarding school would be like. But at least it was a bed! And one that didn't need to be deflated every morning. I lived there for two years. I went from living in a nursery to living in an old-folks home. But none of it mattered to me, because I was living in New York City.

ON THE WAY

I started my internship as soon as I arrived. I didn't want to miss a minute of it, and I also didn't want them to change their minds about hiring the girl from Florida they had never met. The first day I started, I met with the CEO. She was poised, professional, and very sophisticated. I was doing my best to keep it together in one of the two "office-appropriate" looks that my mother had helped me pick out before I left home. The CEO looked me up and down and let out an audible sigh. At the time, I figured my skirt-suit was the problem. I didn't know if interns had a dress code, but I thought a cotton candy knit mock neck tank top and pencil skirt would show the world that I meant serious, professional business. Soon enough I realized that, to her, I was just another fashion hopeful eking through the revolving intern door. I was just another girl who would probably quit when I realized that a design internship didn't mean that I was going to be sitting around all day sketching runway looks and talking about the latest collections from Paris. I was determined to prove her wrong. If I was willing to sleep on a blow-up mattress that I had to inflate and deflate every day, I was willing to do anything and everything they needed me to do in order to prove my worth.

The actual work was pretty anticlimactic. It was not sexy or cool. My first official task was to organize the supply closet. It was just your standard office mess of Post-it Notes, paper clips, and tangled-up extension cords. Junk, basically. But if this was my job, and they were willing to pay me $4.25 an hour, I was going to do it, and I was going to do it well. As I sorted out the stapler refills from the brads and tucked business cards neatly into clear plastic sleeves, I had fantasies of the designer coming up to me and thanking me for my hard work on the closet. He would say that, before I arrived, there had been a lack of order and direction, and now that I was here, he felt like he could really let his creativity flow. That supply closet was impeccable when I finished.

If anyone noticed, they didn't say anything.

I kept showing up for work, and the CEO always had something to keep me busy. I floated around the studio and helped whichever department needed an extra set of hands. I also went to the deli on the corner every day to pick up really important things like toilet paper and Diet Cokes. One day I would be filling orders and shipping boxes at the post office, and the next I would be cataloging fabric swatches. Some days, I didn't do anything fashion- or business related at all. I just did personal errands for the designer or the CEO like dropping off dry cleaning and buying stamps.

I wanted to be a designer, and I understood that this was the first step. I was willing to do whatever it took. I was obsessed with it. I thought about it all the time. Fashion design was my creative calling. I felt like it was the way that I needed to express myself and get my thing—whatever it was going to be—out into the world. This was my purpose. It filled me up and kept me going no matter what. Feeling confident in my purpose is what allowed me to show up for my internship and spend my day organizing swatches.

After six months of doing menial tasks for minimum wage, I was barely getting by. I was willing to keep answering the phone and keep fetching coffees but couldn't keep eating the employees' leftovers or stealing from my geriatric roommates. While I wasn't just another girl from Florida who thought a fashion internship was going to be glamorous, I was determined not to be stuck in the supply closet my entire career. I didn't move to New York to pick up someone's kid from school. I knew I was committed and capable of so much more even if no one else did just yet.

IT'S ABOUT MORE THAN MONEY

Remember when you were little and one of your parents' friends asked you what you wanted to be when you grew up, and you said a ballerina cat? Or maybe you said a super queen or a baby doctor. Your purpose was so simple. You wanted to spread joy through movement. You wanted to be a leader and parade around in a beautiful sparkly cape or care for living things smaller than you. No one sat you down and told you being a ballerina cat wasn't going to pay.

We often shy away from following our dreams because we feel like they won't be able to support us. But when we come from a place of purpose, no matter what we are doing, we walk away full and satisfied.

You don't have to start your own business or run your own company to think this way. It comes down to knowing what you are all about at your core, and then asking yourself if the opportunities that come your way align with your purpose. Maybe you're someone who can talk to anyone and you're the best listener in your friend group. Should you be an accountant and crunch numbers all day because it will pay your bills, or should you look for a customer service job that will put your gift of gab front and center? (And there's nothing wrong with being an accountant, if that's your thing.)

When you design your purpose and not your paycheck, your life becomes about being able to do what you love, not about getting to some arbitrary number in your bank account. Things don't always feel or look the way you thought they would when you get there. A big win at work doesn't mean you're going to quit and spend the rest of your life eating ice cream for break-fast in bed. If you're lucky, you still have to—you still *get to*—wake up and go to work the next day. If you have a successful company, that company does not stop the moment it hits the metrics you've deemed markers of success. That's just the be-ginning, and it's when things start to get fun.

The work is the reward.

Rule #3

DON'T ASK FOR HELP

ask for

what you need

t's true that there are no dumb questions. But it's also true that some questions are way better than others.

Take asking for help, for instance. We hear all the time that you should ask for help when you need it. But how often does asking for help only elicit another question as a response?

Q. "Can you help me?"
A. "How?"

Q. "Can you help me?"
A. "What do you need?"

Q. "Can you help me?
A. "With what?"

Efficient it is not.

My mother always answered my requests for help with more questions. It's probably why my brain was wired early on to think things through from beginning to end. I'd ask myself, *What do I want? Why do I want it? What needs to happen in order to make it happen?* Whatever it was, I would always do as much as I could on my own. Then, if I ran into something that I couldn't figure out, I would decide who to ask, and how and when I was going to ask them. My mother taught me to recognize when I had hit a blockade and wouldn't be able to go any further on my own, and also how to keep things moving right along by knowing what to ask for, who to ask, and how to best approach the subject.

I hit a blockade about six months into my internship. I was getting great experience and was working all the time, but, unsurprisingly, I had no money. It was not the best look for trying to make it in one of the most expensive cities in the world. I didn't just need help. I needed money for obvious reasons.

That winter, flying home for the holidays was not an option. Just the thought of buying a plane ticket to Florida to see my family felt like a complete indulgence, and it was actually impossible given my bank account had eight dollars in it. The CEO felt sorry for me and invited me over to her family's home for dinner. She had taken me under her wing at work, but there wasn't much socializing outside the office. To be invited into her home was kind of a big deal, and I knew this was my chance.

After way too much food and possibly a few too many sneaky sips of wine, I gave her my big pitch on why she should hire me, and I went over all the ways I had proven myself. And then I finally got up the courage to ask her for a job and a raise.

After I made my case, I waited and proceeded immediately to dump buckets of sweat. She remained silent. I kept sweating. Then she said, "You're right. We should hire you. And we will give you a raise." I let out such a huge sigh of relief that spit flew out of my mouth and landed on her blouse. We laughed so hard. It felt like the best night ever, and I consider it, like that original thirty-second phone call, to be one of the experiences that changed the course of my life.

Imagine if I had asked for help. What if I told her my story of barely being able to make it and about the struggle I was having with paying my bills? It would have been uncomfortable. She would have had every reason to say no and regret asking me to her home and making demands. I didn't ask for help. I didn't need charity. I asked for what I wanted and made a case for why I deserved it. And I got it.

KNOW WHAT YOU DON'T KNOW

I'm not an intern anymore, but I know what it's like to work your way up. Here's a question I get asked all the time: Do you have thirty minutes to chat with me about what I might do to get further along in my career?

The short answer is also the truth: No. I honestly can say I do not have thirty minutes to chat with you generally about your career.

It's not that I do not want to. It's just that I don't really know much about you or what it is that you are after, so whatever I would tell you would be generalized advice that may or may not be what you want to hear. Asking business owners how they got started might be inspiring, but their stories will not necessarily apply to you, since everyone has their own path.

Do I have time to talk about things that I look for when I am hiring? Do I have any insight into the pros and cons about producing products domestically versus overseas as a small business? Do I have a second to give you feedback on a possible logo?

Yes. Now we are talking. Literally.

First, you need to know what you need. Only then can you ask for what you want.

We all have that nice friend who seems like the most easygoing person in the world because she never seems to have an opinion about what she wants from the coffee shop or where you should go for dinner. But—and this is a big *but*—this drives me bananas. There could be 450 things on a coffee menu. There are thousands of restaurants in New York City. Wouldn't it make everyone's lives so much easier if we were just specific?

It's easy to send these sorts of asks through email or even a casual direct message. But before you send that email, do your research. Be informed. It will make your entire exchange richer and more useful. Instead of DMing someone you do not know and asking her a question, spend some time going through her world on the web to see if maybe she has already answered it. Chances are that if it's something she gets asked all the time, you'll be able to find the answer somewhere online. You may even find opportunities to connect with the person you're trying to track down, like through a webinar or—shocker—in person.

Not only is doing the research the best way to find the information that you are looking for, but it might lead to a new, more targeted question that will better serve your purpose and make you seem like someone worth talking to. If your question has not been answered somewhere in a public forum, then by all means reach out—just try your best not to take it personally if you don't get a prompt reply or if you get no response at all. And definitely do not hold it against the person you're trying to contact. That would be like getting mad because the busiest person in the room didn't instantaneously drop everything that they are doing in order to start talking to you at the exact moment that you were ready to strike up a conversation.

Here's another way to ask that career-building question, though this version has a much better chance of getting a constructive response: As a boss, what are some of the things employees do that show you they are good candidates for promotion?

Now you're getting somewhere. Be specific with your requests. This approach is going to better serve your purpose for so many reasons. For starters, you're asking me to answer a question from my point of view and from my experience. Whereas with a general question about things that could further your career, I can't tell you what you should do because I don't even know where to start. I don't know what you're capable of, what you're interested in, or what your current situation is at all. When you ask me what it is I am looking for in my team, that I can answer.

Everyone is so damn busy these days. When you have an opportunity to ask someone a question or for a favor—and oftentimes asking for help can be both—don't waste your chance and their time by being vague. What are you really asking for? What do you really need? How can they really be of service to you? Get specific.

When you ask a better question, you get a better answer. So don't ask for help. Ask for what you need.

Rule #4

GIVE YOUR ALL

you have more

to offer than

you might

think

W e all have something to give. And when you discover whatever that thing is, you suddenly feel like you have this bottomless pot of goodness that can go on and on and on.

When I was first finding my way in New York and I didn't know anyone except the few people I worked with and my lovely granny roommates, I started volunteering. There was a nonprofit space that supported up-and-coming artists by hosting gallery nights and live music that was free and open to the public.

For someone with zero friends and even less money (i.e., yours truly), it was a great place to hang out. When I was there, I was surrounded by artists and creativity. I was inspired by the people who, like me, were fearlessly chasing their dreams. I became one of the regulars, so when they needed someone to help organize events, I raised my hand.

I didn't have many resources at that point: I was new in town, I needed all of the little money that I had to cover my basics, and I didn't have a network. The only things I had to offer were time and energy. It's easy to forget that these are two of the most precious resources, and they're also the most accessible. It's up to us how and where we choose to spend them.

Once I got involved, I got *really* involved. Monday through Friday, I would get to the office before 8:00 a.m., sort everything out for my boss, and use any spare time I had to work on ideas for my own collection; then I'd head to the nonprofit space at 3:45 p.m. My only real break was the time it took me to get from the office to the gallery. I would work there until 10:00 at night, answering the phones, checking people in, playing hostess at the nonalcoholic bar, helping the artists set up and clean up, or whatever else needed to be done. I spent my Saturdays and Sundays there too. I kept up my volunteer work for four years, until my business became more demanding—and even then I didn't stop; I just cut down my hours.

I know what you're thinking: Why, when I had a job that paid next to nothing, would I find a gig that paid actually nothing? What a weird way to spend my free time. Why wouldn't I just sleep?

Creative people have always shaped my world. As a child, I found my entertainment and inspiration through the work of dancers, musicians, illustrators, photographers, writers, actors, and designers. If my parents were wondering what I was up to, the options were either dancing around my room to Madonna, sketching bohemian-meets-rock-and-roll looks while listening to Bob Dylan, or curling up to read an amazing work of literary fiction by Judy Blume or Roald Dahl. (Or, even more likely, I was nose-deep in one of the Baby-Sitters Club books. I could never decide if I was more Claudia Kishi because of her personal style or Stacey McGill because she was new in town. It's still up for debate.) Because I saw artists as the people who create and lead our culture, it was a given that I would jump at the chance to be part of their world and vision.

Volunteering didn't have anything to do with my career or my bank account. It made my world a little bit bigger every time I showed up. Giving back filled me up and fueled me to keep going. Not just because I felt like in my own small way I was contributing to the betterment of society as a whole, but because I finally felt part of something. I'd spent plenty of years in Florida feeling like the odd person out. I wasn't having heart-to-hearts back at the apartment with Carol and Margie. But I had finally found people who had similar interests and, even if we were chitchatting as I poured ginger ales, my interactions there gave me a sense of connection in a city that felt so overwhelming a lot of the time.

When my company was just me and an intern, every workday was different, but, no matter what, I showed up for my responsibilities at the nonprofit space. I would arrive with bolts of fabric that I had just picked up in the Garment District and stash them in the back, or I'd come straight from the post office where I had just finished shipping boxes and have just enough time to change in the bathroom. I would put all of my other work aside and be ready to jump in wherever I was needed. It felt good to take a break from thinking about myself, my job, and my problems and focus my attention on something else for a while. The most socializing I ever did was to occasionally go out for dinner with the other volunteers. (On those nights I would crawl into my bed at 2:00 a.m., only to wake up a few hours later to start my day all over again—which now I know is basically the same sleep schedule as when you have a newborn.) It was always worth it. No one made me do it. It just felt right.

Ultimately, I realized that as much as I was giving, I was getting so much more out of it, more than I even imagined I could.

THERE'S A MISSION FOR EVERYONE

There are an infinite number of causes big and small that could use your attention. It can be as small as taking good care of your neighborhood block or beautifying your apartment building. It can be as big as taking a stand for the environment and fighting for a healthier planet. I'm not here to tell you what to care about. Just care about something. I know that when I have shifted my focus away from myself and onto helping others, it has strengthened my connections and expanded my world.

By building giving into your personal and professional lives (which for many of us is basically one and the same), you are being an active and super-important participant in creating a better future for everyone around you.

You have something to offer. You do, or you wouldn't be here.

It's not all about writing a check to make a difference. Financial contributions are one way that people can support causes and organizations that they care about, but there are many others. You don't need to start a foundation in order to have an impact. When you use your ideas, energy, time, skills, and other resources for the greater good, you make the world a better place for everyone, including yourself. Whether it's small actions that you take daily, like sending a postcard to your senator, or big initiatives that take months to coordinate, whatever it is, all that matters is that you do it. Some outreach organizations like food banks or after-school programs can use your time physically. You can go through your closet and donate your old clothing. You can organize a drive with your friends and collect new items to donate to the cause of your choice. You can offer up your time as a professional to a nonprofit that you care about. If you're a graphic designer and you see a nonprofit that could use a face-lift to make a better impression on the world, ask them if they are interested. If you're a writer, you can offer to rewrite their mission statement. And you can always share what you learn and care about with your community. When you speak up about what you care about, you're helping build awareness.

You think all your minutes are spoken for. But then by some miracle, you find an hour to watch *Queer Eye* or Jonathan Van Ness do back handsprings on Instagram. (Which, if you haven't, you should.) When something is important to you, you make time for it.

Always remember that your time is your own. When you're being pulled in many directions, this might not feel like the case, but you are the only one who decides how you're going to spend it. You might have a job, but getting up and actually going every day is a choice. You have obligations, but at the end of the day, whether or not you show up is on you. The truth is that your boss is not making you go to work; you are going to work because you either love it, find some purpose in it, or want to avoid the consequences of not going. Those are all choices. No one is making you go to a birthday dinner even though you don't want to. You are choosing to go because you seriously do not want to deal with the guilt trip from your friend for missing her party. You're not a robot. There's no one hiding in the closet with a remote control.

As an entrepreneur or someone devoted to her professional track, it's easy to operate with blinders on and forget that there is more to life than the to-do list in front of you. But if it's true that we're all in this together, then we all have to do our part, right? Remind yourself of the things that you feel connected to outside of work and adult-life stuff. What do you want to see happening in the world? Where do you want to contribute? How can you incorporate that into your life in a real, doable way?

No matter how busy you think you are, when you decide that giving back is important to you, you will magically find the time you need to do so. Even if it means that you will have less time for yourself or your friends, it won't feel like you're losing anything because you have so much to gain.

Rule #5

POINT OF VIEW IS EVERYTHING

look for the

opportunities

in front of you

How many times have you heard the phrase "What you see is what you get"? Often enough, right? Every time I hear it, it makes me feel like we're supposed to think that what's presented to us is all that there is. We're just supposed to take everything at face value.

The truth is we all have a unique point of view. So if what you see is what you get, it all really depends on how you look at it and what you do with it. You could look at a box of mac 'n' cheese and see dinner. Or you could look at the same box and see pasta beads and orange dye. What you see is what you have to work with.

I've learned to take a good look at what's right in front of me and then switch up my angles. I want to see every possibility. Not just the most obvious one.

I had made it to New York and had landed my first real job in fashion. I was living the dream, albeit with Carol and Margie as roommates. (Nothing gives you the boost of confidence you need to make it in New York City like a sexagenarian checking to see if you made your bed every morning. My form of retaliation was stealing their leftover lentil soup and pasta after they had gone to bed at sunset.) I loved every minute of it. Well, almost every minute of it. Getting lost on the subway while freezing during the winter was a wake-up call. As I started to get more into the energy and flow of NYC, I tried new things, gained ten pounds from eating bagels, learned to love coffee, met new people, and even started to date.

My tastes were very different from those of the designer I worked for. He had established himself as a go-to label for women who loved men's shirts for women, the OG boyfriend shirt. And when I say *boyfriend*, I mean like Richard Gere in *Pretty Woman*, not Sean Penn in *Fast Times at Ridgemont High*. His clients were the uptown sophisticates who shopped at the big-name department stores and dressed for lunch meetings — or more likely just lunch in cream-colored blouses and tailored pants. Maybe you've heard of Craig Taylor? His brand wasn't huge, but it was a successful business with retail accounts across the country and a very loyal fan base. The brand wasn't featured in all of the glossy fashion magazines, but it was respected in the fashion industry. I was grateful. I wanted to understand fit and fabrics and all of the technical aspects. I needed to learn about how to build a brand with a strong foundation from both a business and a collection perspective. Instead of working for someone whose footsteps I wanted to follow, I found myself working for someone who could show me the steps, and then I could make my own way.

Back then, my personal style aspired to be more downtown cool girl, which was less professional and more boho tops and low-rise jeans. (It's okay. Go ahead. I know you're judging. I'm judging me too.) Every day I came to work ready to tackle the to-dos on my boss's list because I knew that once I checked all those boxes, I could sit at my desk and focus on my own collection. After I was finished clipping images and tearing pages from magazines so that I could put together mood boards for my boss that showed fifty shades of beige tailored shirts with forty-five button options, I would go back through those very same mags and tear out pictures of looks that I loved. I took measurements of samples that were on their way to production; I researched resources and hunted down references. I sorted through so many fabric swatches, and I always made two piles: one for work and one for me.

Two years in, I had designed a five-piece collection. This little capsule included a silk blouse (I had translated some of the skills that I had picked up from my boss) with a cummerbund permanently attached, a denim tuxedo (the pants were low-rise with a slight boot-cut flare), a basic T-shirt, and The Shirt that I mentioned earlier. The "look book" itself? Expensive green iridescent paper with metallic binder clips. It had ten shots in the whole entire thing. I felt great about it, except for the fact that in making it I had wiped out my entire savings ($10,000 from summers spent endlessly babysitting and some uncashed bat mitzvah bonds).

READY FOR ANYTHING

By day, I worked. By night, I worked too. While I didn't have the capital to produce anything outside of my five-piece collection, I did have enough money saved to make a few versions of The Shirt (remember, the one that changed everything, or at least put change in motion). Everyone was so into graphic tees that I felt like I needed to have one in this collection, but I didn't have the money to make my own shirts or screen blank tees. The cheapest option was to buy the existing tops and make them my own. My inspiration for it, as mentioned before, was that escapist energy of a tourist beach T-shirt—think of those acid-washed neon tees available up and down the Atlantic coast or those island-style tanks customized with fringe and beads, which I had fallen for during my first trip to the Caribbean. I wanted to take that energy and make it cool, make it about my new home. I had been cutting up and knotting T-shirts since my dance-class days back in middle school, so taking a tee from basic and boring to meet-me-at-the-barre with a trusty pair of scissors was second nature to me.

Whenever I had the chance, I would play around with different techniques of cutting, tying, and customizing the T-shirts. I really tried everything: asymmetrical necklines, asymmetrical hemlines, asymmetrical sleeves; cutting sleeves off, tying them back on, cutting them shorter. I couldn't afford to let any shirt go to waste, so if one came out a little odd, I'd keep playing around with it until it worked. (Some would get cut and reshaped, getting smaller and smaller, so many times that I was worried I'd have to start a kids' line.) I wore one myself and gave them away to a few friends. Today, that would be called marketing. Back then, it was just thrilling to have something that I made worn by a person other than myself outside of my apartment.

One of the people I gave a T-shirt to was my then friend, now sister-in-law, Stephanie. She's just one of those people who can wear anything and look amazing. One night in Los Angeles, Steph threw on the shirt with a pair of jeans and a blazer and headed out to Chi Dynasty in Los Feliz for dinner with her friend Jenna Elfman. Jenna asked if Steph could get her a shirt. Of course Dharma of the early aughts hit sitcom *Dharma & Greg* could have a shirt! I was such a big fan that I sent it to her the very next day. It was September 9, 2001.

It was around this time that I was introduced to a publicist who had just started out. We met through mutual friends and hit it off. We met up at Cafe Gitane after work, and I showed him my look book. I was dying for his feedback. All he really said was that he felt like there was something "interesting" there. I couldn't tell what he meant by that. *Interesting* can go either way. But a few weeks after meeting, he got in touch to let me know he was curating a small group show of emerging designers, and he asked if I would like to participate. The answer was a big, resounding yes. It would be at a gallery in Chelsea. At the time it felt like a big deal. The audience consisted of the super high-powered fashion elite: my parents and the parents of the other designers. The show was on September 10, 2001.

Early the next morning on September 11, still on a high from the show the night before, I went to a fabric seminar to learn about cotton. It was a trend forecast talking about the future of the most timeless fabric around. I mostly went to those things to network and meet people and try to get access to fabric at wholesale costs. It seemed like just another day. Before the presenter even took the stage, the organizer ran in, so upset, and announced that there had been an attack on the World Trade Center.

The 9/11 tragedy rocked the city, the country, and the world.

My boss called to make sure I was safe. We weren't going to go into work that day, and we probably wouldn't be going for a little while. We had no idea of the extent of what had happened or how the events would play out. I checked in with friends from the nonprofit where I volunteered and heard they were headed to a site that was helping the first responders. Against the stream of people headed north, I walked my way downtown until I found the high school–turned–emergency center in Tribeca where my friends were. I didn't know what to do with myself, so I pitched in however I could: finding places for people to sit, handing out water, trying to be of service. Helping others has always helped me: taking action and doing something to help other people helps me process my feelings; it's my therapy.

New York and New Yorkers are nothing if not resilient. After a few weeks, despite the devastation and heartbreak, people were continuing to come together and starting to find new rhythms in that new normal. I continued to make my way to the volunteer site daily, just doing whatever needed to be done. My fashion show felt like it had happened in another lifetime. As much as I had hoped that some important editor would have noticed me or that I would have been the breakout star of the show that night, I put all of those feelings aside.

In early October, my phone rang. It was Jenna Elfman's assistant calling to let me know that Jenna had filmed a segment for *The Tonight Show* with Jay Leno. She had worn the I Heart New York shirt that I had customized for her on the show. It was going to air that night. It seemed surreal. I couldn't let myself believe it until I saw it with my own eyes. I tuned in that night and there it was: a white T-shirt with the iconic graphic that I had slashed, snipped, shredded, fringed, knotted, tied, and sewn back together into the ultimate tribute to the city that the whole world loved.

The Shirt was truly an homage to the city that I had idealized and dreamed about from afar. It had welcomed me, my dreams, and my crappy old suitcases with its inspiration, palpable energy, and endless possibilities. The 9/11 tragedy broke my heart, but I was grateful I had created something to celebrate my new hometown, even if it was as trivial as a customized tee that banded people together and lifted their spirits.

If someone had told me what would happen next, I would have never believed them.

I got fired.

The morning after Jenna wore The Shirt on TV, I woke up to a ringing phone and an inbox full of messages. For the first time in my life, people wanted to buy something that I had made. I had to pinch myself more than once. A day later, all of the popular gossip weeklies ran shots of Jenna from the show, and the demand grew tenfold. I needed some I Heart New York shirts, and I had to get down to customizing them fast.

Between volunteering and tracking down more and more T-shirts to meet the demand, I was barely sleeping. The office had been closed since the attacks, so when my phone rang and it was the CEO, I figured she was calling to tell me they were ready to get back to business as usual. I gave her the full update, told her everything that was happening with my line: the buyers who had called, the magazines that had covered it, the editors who wanted to meet, and the celebrity requests that had started to come in. She seemed genuinely happy for me. And then, to wrap things up, she said: "Just so you know, you're fired." Um. Okay. I felt like a Ping-Pong ball that was being launched back and forth between extreme highs and unprecedented lows. "You know what you need to do, so it's time you go do that. I'm here for you," she told me.

Some people might have seen that moment as the end. I have always looked at it as the beginning. That was the start of Rebecca Minkoff as you know it today.

DIY IRL

After Jenna wore my shirt on *The Tonight Show*, I turned into a full-time T-shirt-customization machine. I rode all over the city—to Times Square, through Chinatown—to every tourist kiosk, buying as many T-shirts as possible: five for eighty dollars here, two for thirty there. Twenty for one hundred dollars at one memorable stop. I honestly believe that I have bought more I Heart New York T-shirts than anyone else in the whole entire world. I scanned, saved, and printed every mention that I got in any magazine. I had made a list of the boutiques that I thought were incredibly cool, and then I printed out my line sheets and press kit and hand-delivered them to each store. A few shops placed orders or took a few shirts on consignment. Every time I got a new order, it felt like another piece of the puzzle falling into place.

In order to make sure that these pieces didn't just sit on the racks and that people actually bought them, I had postcards printed with a picture of The Shirt and the addresses of where it could be found. I was one of those people who would stand in Union Square for hours passing out postcards to college kids and tourists. Most people blew past me like they had big, important things to do, which they probably did. I assumed they were residents. Some of the people asked me if I knew the designer. My answer really depended on their vibe. It did not feel good to see my name trampled on the sidewalk at the end of the day—I ain't gonna lie—but all of that promotion worked, because my stuff sold.

TIMING IS EVERYTHING

My friend Patrick became my official publicist. He was my lifeline to the magazine world. His friend Jill ran an online store called Raven Style. These were the early days of e-commerce. Back then, if you were direct-to-consumer, the general opinion was that you couldn't afford to have a brick-and-mortar shop. Today, we see DTC as a revolutionary business model that has disrupted industries over and over again.

Webshops were primitive. You were lucky if you had one semi-decent image, a product description without any typos, and an add-to-cart button that worked. People weren't obsessed with optimizing user experience and options. Adding filters so you could narrow down your results constituted serious bells and whistles. Online shopping was a whole new frontier, which made it exciting even if the process was imperfect and slow, slow, slow.

Jill and I immediately hit it off. Thanks to The Shirt and the attention it had received, editors had heard of my name. That was the part that truly mattered. When they called my publicist's office asking if he had anything to fit a nautical story or a spring accessories roundup, he would dig a little deeper into what exactly they were looking for. Then my phone would ring, and he would say so-and-so is looking for a terry-cloth jumpsuit or a jersey dress in this shade of mint or a denim miniskirt. I'd say okay, hop on my bike, find the fabric and finishings I needed, ride back to my apartment, sit at my sewing machine, and make whatever it was that they had requested. I would drop it off at his office the next morning, and he would send it off to the photo shoot.

If the piece was confirmed to be featured in the magazine, then it would be added to the e-commerce site. When a style took off, Jill would place her orders in multiples of five, and other buyers would get in touch too. Back then, people were more into one-offs, and definitely more forgiving of homemade-looking stuff, but I wanted pieces to be polished and consistent, so I turned production over to a very talented and dependable sewer. His operation was a one-stop shop from sketch to garment production. We had met while I was making the rounds of the Garment District.

• • •

WAS I HAVING FUN? Yes. Could I pay my bills? No way. Absolutely not. I just couldn't figure out the economics. Even though I was working around the clock, I needed a job. One that paid actual money.

On top of everything, I was itching to find a new living situation for obvious reasons. Desperate to get out—and fully convinced that it would lead to an epic romance—I decided to force a guy that I had been seeing to move into an itty-bitty apartment with me on the Upper West Side. A week before moving in, the flame fizzled. Not only did he break my heart—every guy seemed like The One until it was very clear he wasn't—he left me without a place to live: Carol had already rented my room out.

At this point, I had been in New York for four entire years, and I hadn't molded a career on which I could completely support myself. I was working tirelessly, but it seemed like I wasn't getting anywhere. So, after this big breakup, which felt very end-of-the-world at the time, when my parents told me to come home, I didn't say no right away. I'll never forget the day when my mother said, "Maybe now this is the time to come back, regroup, and figure out what you want to do with your life."

It seemed like I had two choices in front of me:

A. A cool apartment in New York that I could not afford
B. My childhood bedroom in Florida that was free

Neither one was the right option for me, so I needed to create a third, which ultimately wasn't the right path either. I had all of New York City in front of me, and I was going to figure it out. Through a friend of a friend of a friend, I managed to sublet a room during two of the hottest months I can remember. There was no air-conditioning. No window that would open. I wasn't allowed to go into the general living area because my roommate said my rent only covered my bedroom and "occasional" bathroom use. I had a lot of reasons to get out of there fast.

Through a cool girl at the nonprofit, I found a place in SoHo, on Thomspon and Spring. The neighborhood was a cache of the New York City lifestyle that I had dreamed about. The apartment was tiny, the bedroom I was renting was miniscule, but I was living the dream. I squeezed in a twin mattress that I had found leaning up against a street-cleaning sign on a fancy block in the West Village and propped it up on milk crates from the mom-and-pop corner store so that I could store things underneath. The night I moved in, I sat on the fire escape just like they do in the movies. As I looked out over the dirty street, I felt like I had made it. I was a designer who lived in SoHo. I was a designer. Who lived in SoHo! Maybe even one day I would be able to afford dinner at Da Silvano.

This feeling was short-lived. I was always late on rent. It was clear that this was not a situation that could last. I ended up finding a much more affordable spot on the way-less-glamorous Lower East Side. Though it was less per month than my spot in SoHo, it was still a stretch, but I needed to make it work. So I hauled my bed and milk crates across Broadway and made myself as comfortable as possible. Which wasn't actually that comfortable (milk crates don't make a great bed frame), but it was better than giving up and moving home.

The truth was that if I was going to get by in New York City, I needed a side hustle to support my actual hustle. Jenna had a friend who was directing a commercial and looking for a stylist. (If it's starting to sound like Jenna is my fairy godmother, that's because it's true.) I knew what a stylist was, but I didn't really understand what that entailed. The pay was $1,000 a day, so I said yes. I knew I would figure it out as I went.

Thankfully, it turned out that I was pretty competent when it came to getting other people dressed. The work wasn't predictable or very consistent, but when it paid, it paid well. The money that I made picking up random gigs like styling Heidi Klum for the very first season of *Project Runway* or Padma Lakshmi for *Top Chef* really bridged the gap. There was no luxury though. There was no going out to dinner. I wasn't barhopping and treating everyone to drinks. Everything I made went to cover my living expenses and back into my line. And somehow I still managed to rack up $60,000 in credit card debt. That's New York City for you.

Logically, it made no sense for me to keep doing what I was doing, but that is where passion stepped in to save the day. It wasn't about the money (or lack thereof); I just couldn't stop. I was totally obsessed with fashion and design. It was how I expressed myself in the world. I thought about it all the time. I just had to do it. Some might have looked at my situation and seen a million reasons to bail, but all I could see were reasons to keep at it. I was doing it on my own, which meant I was calling my own shots. I was in debt (so much debt!), but the only way I would be able to ever pay it off was if I started making money, and to do that I needed to work. I hadn't officially "made it." But I believed I had, because I got to do my dream job in the city that I loved.

What you see is what you get, right?

Rule #6

LOVE IT AND LEAVE IT

be okay with

walking away

T hree years into my business, I was barely getting by. My collection was doing decent, but I was still taking every styling job I could get to pay the bills.

On one of our sales trips out to Los Angeles, I had a dinner date with Jenna. We were catching up at Chi Dynasty over chicken in lettuce cups (if ya know, ya know), and she told me all about a movie she was working on that had just started pre-production. She asked if I did bags. I said of course. Which was absolutely not true. I had never made a bag in my life, and she needed it in a week. Perfect.

I headed back to New York the next day and got to work. This wasn't something that I could whip up in my room by myself. A homemade tote bag was not going to cut it. It had to be unique. It had to be quality. This bag would be in a movie, and there was no room for error. I started sketching out what I thought the perfect bag of the moment could be. At the time, everyone was into the Fendi Spy Bag and Chloe Paddington, and I didn't want to do something derivative of what was already on the shelves, out in the streets, and in the magazines. I had to think outside of the box—or the bag, in this case.

In those days, it was all about the *Sex and the City* lifestyle: serendipitous meetings on the subway, romantic encounters on the street, getting past the velvet rope to dance the night away—and having a handbag with room for your dancing shoes when you headed off to work the morning after a wild night out (sleep felt really optional in those days). And just like that, the idea of the Morning After Bag was born. Now I had to make that idea a reality.

Once I had my sketch in hand, I needed to bring it to life. I went to source materials and asked all of my vendors who was the best of the best to work with and the worst of the worst to avoid. When it came to producing a bag, I really had no clue where to start, but I was familiar enough with the factory world to tell the good guys from the jokers. I made appointments for that day.

At my first factory meeting, I put my idea on the table. The man on the other side was a tall, austere Russian who was so quiet it was intimidating. After I went over my sketches with him, he said, "Give me a second," and he walked out with a very confident swagger. When he came back, he had a bag in his hand. "Do you know what this is?" he asked. Of course I did. It was every downtown cool girl's ultimate bag of the moment. He continued, "This is what I make." I honestly couldn't believe my eyes. "No you don't," I said. "That's a knockoff." And with that, he turned around, walked back to the door, and motioned for me to follow him.

He walked me through the factory, pointing out the heavy-duty sewing machines and industrial riveters. I started noticing familiar colors of leather and caught a glimpse of a couple pieces of hardware that seemed vaguely familiar. As we got closer to the end of the production line, I saw the It Bag of the moment coming together piece by piece, stitch by stitch. New York's hottest bag was being manufactured right in front of my face. I felt like I had struck gold. If this guy could make those bags, he could definitely make mine. I gave him my sketch and my last $1,600. He told me to come back in a week.

The next seven days were a real roller coaster. All I could think about was what was happening at the factory. I imagined my new Russian friend painstakingly cutting each canvas panel by hand, surrounded by sewers watching his every move. (I'm sure this didn't happen.) I would call to check in to see how everything was going. He would get on the phone and, in his very thick, very rough Russian accent, tell me it was going "Goot. Really goot."

Around day four, I wanted to stop by to see the progress, but he told me that was not necessary and he would call me when it was ready. On day seven, he told me to call tomorrow and that the bag should be ready for me then. He said the same thing the next day and the day after that. I was forcing myself not to panic. I still had a chance, but I could feel my window of opportunity closing. If I didn't get the bag to Los Angeles before they started shooting the scene, all of this was going to be for nothing. Worst of all, I'd be letting my friend down who had done so much for me. I had never made a bag, and I didn't know the process or how and when to push. On day ten, I got the call.

My first Morning After Bag was chocolate brown canvas with metallic faux crocodile trim and a turquoise zipper. To me it was perfect. But it was also technically three days late. I rushed to the factory, rushed to FedEx, and packed the bag on the spot. I overnighted it the fastest, most expensive way possible to LA and started praying that it would make it into her hands by the time they started shooting. I was awake all night checking the delivery status. Whenever my phone rang, I held my breath, hoping it would be Jenna's assistant. When it was finally her on the other end of the line, I could tell that something wasn't right from the way that she said hello. Her tone was a mix of having a heavy heart and genuine annoyance: the bag wasn't there and they started filming with another bag. And no, they wouldn't reshoot it. And no, they were not going to have her carry a second bag anywhere else in the film. The bag arrived two hours later. The bag was late. It missed its big moment. And so had I.

I was devastated. Not only did that opportunity go up in flames, but that was also the last of the money I had to my name. I missed my chance to become an internationally recognized bag designer. These kinds of chances didn't come along twice, and the feeling in the pit of my stomach at the lost opportunity was truly painful. I went over every day, every minute, every choice that I had made that had led to this royal screwup. I counted all the ways where I could have pushed harder and been clearer, all the things I had let fall through the cracks.

I had no savings and no one I could borrow money from. My credit cards were maxed out, and my family was kind of over me. We were raised to be independent self-starters, so all of my not-so-subtle hints at floating me a little extra cash to get by as I chased my fashion-designer dreams were not getting me anywhere. So I did what anyone would do if they were stuck with a $1,600 two-of-a-kind purse: I put all my stuff in it and brought it everywhere with me.

People started freaking out. In a good way.

Everyone loved it. I couldn't go out without someone stopping me in the street to ask who made it and where they could get one. I showed it to my friend Ilaria, who was the buyer for a store in Los Angeles called Satine. She ordered twelve for the shop. It might not seem like a dozen bags is that big of a deal, but to me it was. There were materials to source, factories to find, and production to figure out. And most importantly, I needed to figure out where things had gone wrong before and make sure not to repeat the same mistakes. At $600 a pop, this wasn't a small amount that they were investing in me. They were willing to take a gamble.

I was on a mission. Back to my factory friend I went. I mixed and matched neutral canvas colors with textured leather and tracked down bright zippers to make the MAB stand out. I wanted a woman to smile every time she looked at her bag. It was lined with vintage fabric because I thought you should always open up your bag and feel happy. When the bags came in, Ilaria showed them to her friend, who was an editor at Daily-Candy. Back then, there were two things that made you: Oprah (duh) and DailyCandy, one of the early daily email newsletters. While many publications were already relying on celebrities to give their stamp of approval before featuring a new style or young designer, DailyCandy just wanted to be first. The day that DailyCandy featured the MAB, Satine sold all twelve bags by lunchtime and ordered seventy-five more by dinner.

That's when I started to sweat. I didn't have the money to put that many bags into production. I called my dad and asked for a loan. He said no. As I mentioned, he and my mom weren't the type of parents who would float me financially. During my first few years in NYC, they had helped me secure a credit card and loaned me money here or there to cover absolute essentials. But this didn't feel like one of those life-or-death situations. He told me to call my brother Uri.

I called Uri. He didn't say no. He had a few thousand questions to ask me. This whole handbag thing had come out of the blue. He thought I'd been focused on clothing. What was happening with the clothing business anyway? How was I going to make clothing and bags when both were costly to produce? What sort of bag was I even making? What was Satine? Were they sure they could sell through? What would happen if they did? What would happen if they didn't? Did I know if I was going to be able to get enough material? Where would the bags be made? Take all of these queries and multiply them by a thousand, and you have an idea of just how fast my brother's mind works. If I'm the creative one, he's the supercomputer. I definitely did not have all the answers. I also didn't have much of a backup plan if he said no.

Eventually, after talking through the entirety of the proposition, Uri said yes. He would loan me $2,500 to make this next round of bags.

THE GREAT PIVOT

Round after round of orders kept rolling in. With the success of the bag, Satine invited me to join their new showroom. The MAB was the bag that everyone wanted, so instead of messing with the design, I offered it in forty different colors. It was the ideal shape and weight for an everyday bag that looked as cool when it was just used for carrying around your phone, keys, and wallet as it did when you stuffed a dress in too. Now, its signature combo of canvas, leather, and statement hardware was easy to spot in the street. It was light enough to lug around, but it felt constructed and substantial.

When I designed the bag, I just designed a bag that I loved. It wasn't much deeper or more philosophical than that. It was the bag that I needed and that I imagined other women needed too. It was a bag that could work for every phase of your day and night, at the time in your life when you own one bag. It needed to be there for every moment. Today, we imagine what sort of life a bag will take on when someone reaches for it—if it needs to be hands-free, or how many pockets it should have and what will go into those pockets. Back then, all a bag had to do was just sit there and look pretty.

MEANWHILE, MY CLOTHING LINE was sitting on the sidelines.

It was the sort of thing where someone would call about the MAB and have endless hours to discuss the particulars, the hardware, and the trim, but the second I brought up the clothing line they suddenly had to go. Honestly, I was getting tired of the struggle. It was creatively satisfying to design these things that I knew I wanted to wear, and that my friends said they loved and wanted to wear, too, but it was like I was the only one who saw the magic in it. The easy success of the MAB gave me a fresh perspective on all the work that I had done to keep the clothing line afloat. It was like the MAB had been sprinkled with magic fairy dust and the clothing line was collecting cobwebs.

You can think you have the best business idea in the world, but if it's not profitable or showing any signs of being profitable, cut your losses and move on. Instead of banging your head against the wall trying to force something to work, freeing yourself from it allows you the time and space to think of new ideas and try new things that might work way better.

I made the decision to drop the clothing line. It was something I started, my clothing line that I loved and had built my career on, but the facts were the facts, and they weren't adding up in my favor. Admitting that it was failing and that no one wanted it felt like admitting that I had failed and no one wanted me. It was really hard. But so was feeling broke all the time.

Out of necessity, I realized that if I wanted to make my business work, I was going to need to follow the momentum. Business was easier with the bag, and the purpose that I found in designing clothing had receded to the point where I knew I needed to let it go. Now, I was finding purpose in creating an item that people wanted. Ultimately, my goal was to create items that made women feel good about themselves and that gave them the confidence boost so many of us needed.

The bag was like a magnet for attention. Interest for the bag was constantly flowing our way while the clothing required this sort of exhausting nonstop sales pitch that never quite seemed to click. If clothing was my first love, then handbags were my hot new flame. Creatively, I had found a new way to express myself and put beautiful things into the world. The only difference was that now people really wanted what I was putting out there.

IF THERE'S ONE aspect of your life, work, or project that seems like it's really working, pay attention. It might not be the obvious one or the one that you always imagined it would be, but if it's working and working for you, focus on it. See where it goes.

Today, it's so common for an entrepreneur or a company to change directions that it's just called pivoting. It's not seen as a bad thing. It's seen as a smart move. It means that whoever is in charge is paying enough attention to know what's working and what's not—it means that their ego isn't too wrapped up in the business and they are capable of being objective. Big tech companies now have failure funnels. They come up with ideas, build them, and test them out, and what works keeps going and what doesn't goes in the trash. There's no feeling of sadness. They don't berate themselves. The ideas are experiments. They learn from them and move on. It's okay if they don't work out. On to the next. You can do that too.

Don't take it personally if something doesn't work. Don't beat yourself up if you decide you need to go in a different direction. Acknowledge the reality of the situation and take the emotion out of it. Every minute you spend stuck on the hamster wheel of why something didn't go exactly as you had planned is a minute you could be spending on creating something new.

Rule #7

BE BETTER TOGETHER

practice with
partnerships
makes perfect

Working partnerships take, well, work.

My brother Uri is the CEO and cofounder of Rebecca Minkoff the brand. And as you know, he was my first investor. (Well, technically, our dad was the first investor, but it wasn't by choice. He was the guarantor on my credit card, and I had racked up $60,000 in debt. I wasn't really able to pay him back until 2012, and when I did, I did so with interest. So that counts, right?)

After I called Uri to see if he would loan me the money to produce the first bags, he became the person I called with all my business questions. Uri was already running a successful software business of his own. Through our many, many conversations, it was becoming really, really obvious that I needed help. Design, marketing, and public relations came naturally to me. I knew what people wanted to wear, and I could bring it to life. I loved getting the word out. I loved trying new and different ways of marketing myself and my wares. But business logistics and

financial models? Those were not my thing. Neither were cost-
ing out potential offerings or setting up supply chains. Or all of
the other things that involved spreadsheets that I didn't know
how to make or lawyers with paperwork in legalese that I didn't
know how to speak.

DEFINE YOUR RELATIONSHIPS

Not every entrepreneur needs or wants a partner. There are
many people out there who prefer to be the only one in charge.
It's important to them that every decision be their own. It's not
that they are doing every single ounce of work themselves; it's
that they want to have the final word. And they don't need to
worry about arguing to get their way. It's always their way.

As the bags became more popular, the business began to
bloom. As the business grew, the time that Uri and I spent on
the phone grew too. We were basically talking on the phone all
of the time. And if we weren't talking, we were texting and
emailing. Soon, he started coming up from Florida to work with
me in person once a month. During these visits, we would
power through as much as we could face-to-face. Not long after
he started making the trip north, he started coming up twice a
month; then he started to stay for a few days at a time. After a
few long years of going back and forth, he and his family packed
up and moved to New York. It was a slow slide into a full-on
partnership. There was no denying that he had a business savvy
and financial mindset that complemented my skills. It was key
to have a partner so that I could focus on what I do best.

In the beginning, we really stayed in our lanes. I was responsible for the creative, and he was behind the scenes making it
happen. I relied on my brother to make all business decisions.
I often told him, "You're the CEO; you seem to know this. I'll

focus on design." And at one point he looked at me—and I still hate admitting when he's right—and he said, "You need to evolve. You can't just be the designer in your ivory tower. You have to learn this. This is a language and a way of being." And so I resentfully started diving in and getting myself educated.

It was a lot of pretending in the beginning. In our board meetings, I would be looking up words under the table: *What is EBITDA? What's an* adjusted *EBITDA?!* And I'd often think, *Well, they know that I don't know, so they'll just ask those questions to my brother.* But I didn't like feeling that way. I didn't like not knowing what the board members were talking about or the intricate details of a complicated global brand. I knew I had to learn this stuff.

KNOW YOUR LANE

Once we got more comfortable with our roles, we started crossing over into each other's turf, and that's when the fireworks started. We had many years of it being just awful. We fought constantly. We fought about who was more dedicated to the company and who got to do all the fun stuff.

Seems like a recipe for disaster pie, doesn't it?

Clear boundaries and direct communication have saved us. It's what's given us the ability to hang on to each other during this wild ride.

Effective communication doesn't happen by accident. It might be easier for some people than others, and it can be heavily influenced by interpersonal dynamics and relationships, but it's worth all of the effort and then some.

To solve our issues, the first thing we did was accept that we speak different languages. We see things differently. We prioritize things differently. We're just different people. Period. Even if it doesn't always feel like it, I value and respect his opinion, and I know the feeling is mutual. This is often why we find ourselves in a deadlock: He's got a valid point; I've got a valid point. Neither one of us really wants to hear it. One of us has to be valid-er (in this case, for example, I would lose for using a made-up word). As much as I hate his stubbornness when it's directed toward me, it is this exact quality—when it's directed toward others—that has kept the business going.

We decided we needed a mediator. Getting a neutral party involved when you and your partner, colleague, or friend keep having the same conversation but are finding it impossible to come to a new conclusion can help move things along. For a while, we went to our dad. He knew us both well and would understand where we were coming from, and this, hopefully, would help us get our side heard and understood by the other. It worked for a little while, but it was too easy to let this get personal and emotional. It wasn't great for our family dynamic. Now we work with a mediator who can come into the conversation with a truly neutral point of view and who won't bring up things that we did when we were in high school.

SPEAK EASY

Learning to be a good communicator myself has required real dedication and strategy. Why can't everybody read my mind? It seems so easy! Wink, wink. I slowed down and finally realized that even though it was obvious to me what I had going on, the type of changes that needed to be made, or the next steps that should be taken, I needed to let other people in on this information in a way that made sense to them. Before I committed to working on my communication skills, I took all that for granted.

I've learned to take a moment or two to prep myself before an interview, sales call, negotiation, or any meeting to ask myself what the purpose is and what my goals are. How do I get my message from Point A (me) to Point B (the other person)? It's a simple framework, but it's effective. What do I want to get across? Once I have that clarified, I can work through all of the ways that I can articulate my ideas. How much context does the person I'll be speaking with need in order to understand what I have to say? What's our relationship? Can I speak freely and drop the F-bomb, or do I need to watch my language? At what point will this person jump into the conversation? I always think about what sort of impression I want to give and what sort of takeaway I want to leave, and I strive to nail down clear next steps if need be.

We're all trying to be heard and understood on every level. At work, it's the first step. Communicating in a way that gives people a full, accurate understanding of us is an equally important goal. Once I have your attention, I must set the intention to get my message across clearly. There's no room for gray areas in business. If things are clear, you will get the outcome that you want; if things are confusing, your outcome will likely be messy.

The worst thing that anyone can say to me is, "There was a miscommunication." That means that, at some point, we were having a conversation and we just stopped understanding each other. So, in every meeting, in every Zoom with my team, I'm constantly scanning for nodding heads. Is everyone aligned? Are there any questions?

Be clear on where everyone stands and when you need to tweak your approach to make sure it's understood. There will likely be a lot of trial and error; during my company's early years, this required constant attunement. Now, most days, I do it without thinking. I don't want to leave anyone behind.

The key to all of this is clarity. I aspire to be direct and to the point. It took years for me to get comfortable with being straightforward. There's an expectation that, as women, we're supposed to use smiley faces and exclamations all the time and that, if we don't, something must be wrong, like our feelings are hurt or we are mad about something. In the past, I might have prefaced my feedback on a campaign with questions like, *Do you think this will resonate?* and *Should we try this idea instead?* But I've learned that you can't run a business that way. Your team needs direction. Today, I'll say, *Thank you for this! Here's what I think, and here's what I would adjust. What does everyone think? Great, let's go.* Honest feedback doesn't imply that an idea is bad or that you don't value someone's contribution. You're catalyzing the process, inviting perspectives, and pushing projects forward. What's worse than five people sitting around a table when none of them want to make a decision? That's the IRL version of progress being stopped in its tracks.

When you're trusting others to tell your story, make it short and sweet. It's like a game of telephone. If you start out with "Let's build a collection around the feeling of *Roman Holiday* but set to a 'Material Girl'–type soundtrack," and then you get back Madonna-goes-to-Domino's Pizza, there's an issue. Being succinct is crucial on a team.

It's also important to be aware of people's triggers and not to push their buttons, no matter how tempting it may be. Even if you think something is a silly nonissue. If it's a big deal to them, it should be a big deal to you. And it's even more important not to push people intentionally, no matter how frustrated or infuriated they may make you. If you know that your partner hates it when people tell her to relax, just don't do it. It might seem like a trifling little thing to you, but to her, it's a thing. Respect that. Not only because it's being a conscientious colleague, but also because once you push her buttons, your whole mission goes off the rails. One moment you're only wishing she were not so heated about the possibility of missing a shipping deadline, but then you pull the trigger on the "relax" bomb, and the next moment you are in for a whole tirade on everything that is wrong with the way the business is going and what got you into the position of missing a possible ship date in the first place. This is not what you want. You want solutions.

Start by looking inward to discover who you really are, and then try to be that way with everyone you interact with. For me, no longer overthinking things or being afraid to share what's on my mind helps me feel more confident being myself.

Knowing your weaknesses is just as important as knowing your strengths. Once you can articulate your shortcomings or regular challenges as a business owner, you will be able to communicate your needs clearly and connect with the right people to support you, whether that is a partner, employee, or consultant.

The same reason professional partnerships can be hard is the same reason that they can work: you and your partner are different. In the most effective partnerships, those involved have complementary skill sets. Before committing to a working relationship, you may want to ask yourself the following questions:

Do you and your potential partner have complementary skill sets, or are you good at the same things?

Do you want to be in constant contact with that person all the time? Even on nights and weekends?

Do you want a stakeholder who is financially and emotionally committed to the success of the business, or do you want an employee who is free to come and go?

Do you want someone to be up with you in the middle of the night when things go wrong, or do you want someone who goes back to his or her life at the end of the day?

When Uri and I clearly defined our roles and left each other alone to do our respective jobs, that's when we found our groove. I love design, and that is what I am good at. I don't need to walk into Uri's office and demand to know why someone is or isn't getting paid. As the founder, I want to know what's going on in every part of the business so that I can make the best decisions possible, but I also need to trust that people are going to be doing their jobs—and doing them well.

Once Uri and I defined our roles as business partners, we also needed to define our roles as siblings. Our families do not want to hear about how bad the leather supplier messed up or about all the new hires we need to make. We are colleagues while we are at work, and we are siblings when we get home. Respecting those boundaries is the only way we'll make it for the long haul.

Good communication isn't just about tactics. It's about authenticity. Now, that's the real work.

Rule #8

COMMUNICATE YOUR HEART OUT

dialogue

daily to stay

in sync

F or effective communication, being able to say what you mean and process what you hear is crucial. But when it comes to good communication, a willingness to put yourself out there and be vulnerable can mean the difference between watercooler chitchat that no one remembers and a life-changing conversation.

If you took a snapshot of my business in 2005, you would see me and an intern attempting to fulfill the orders for a whopping total of seventy bags in the tiny apartment we used as a live/work space in a no-elevator building just east of Union Square. Just thinking about those stairs makes me break into a sweat.

On one of my rare purely social outings with my friend Brie, she told me she wanted to set me up with some guy she knew. When it came to dating, I was always looking to get serious, but that approach and New York City in your twenties doesn't mix. My love life was starting to feel like a made-for-TV rom-com (one so bad and cliché that it wasn't even considered for theatrical release). I was seriously starting to worry that there were only losers out there. But from Brie's description, this mystery man sounded promising: he was an actor who was in a band and was funny, nice, good-looking—all the things you want to hear. The only two issues were that he lived in Los Angeles and had a girlfriend. I filed Brie's idea under "it's the thought that counts" and pretended like she had never brought it up.

Fast-forward six months to me, fresh off a plane and in a car in Los Angeles. I was heading toward an ex-boyfriend's house for a reunion that I was sure would end in a proposal of marriage (if not that night, then definitely one day). For way too many years in a row, my phone would ring on New Year's Eve and it would be him on the other end of the line professing his undying love for me, which would always end with me convincing him to give "us" one more shot. It became like an annual drunk dial. On our last exchange, he had been particularly heavy on the Love You part. I fell for it as I had every year before. I didn't even know how much of a sucker I really was until I called him from the car leaving the airport that day to say that I was on my way over. To which he responded, "Yeah, so, now's not a great time. I have company over." And by "company" he meant a woman. So, change of plans: my romantic quest was canceled immediately and indefinitely, and instead I would be going to see my parents, who had recently moved back to California and settled in Los Angeles. (I know the goal of this book is to empower you to overcome your fears and make strong, clear choices as you create your unique path through this world, but, let me just say, when your ex calls on New Year's Eve, let it go to voice mail, no matter how much champagne you've had. Bad idea.)

TIME TO TAKE STOCK

After letting myself in and making myself comfortable in my parents' guest room, I did that thing that people say to do when you're seeking to get clarity about what it is you really want: I wrote it down. Whether it's connected to your career, home, partner, or any area of your life, taking the time to articulate what it is that you want, as well as all of the things that you don't want, helps get you off the hamster wheel in your brain and move forward. When you're clear about what you're looking for, you'll know it when you see it.

I had always been able to articulate what I wanted creatively or in regards to work, but I had never taken the time to really think about what I wanted in a romantic partner. With not much else going on, I decided to make a list while I hung out in my parents' guest bedroom and waited for someone, anyone, to call me and invite me to do something, anything. My list started out with the basics: I wanted a man who was honest, trustworthy, ambitious, funny . . . you know, the stuff that all decent human beings seem to have in common. Since I had nothing but time and had a very fresh impression of what I didn't want, I got really specific with my adjectives: brown hair, green eyes, Jewish or "Jew-ish" (I would even settle for someone who could hum along to Hanukkah songs), someone who would describe himself as an artist . . . The list ended up being really, really long.

Finally my phone rang. It was Karen (the good kind of Karen). She was taking me to a friend's house party up in the Silver Lake hills. It was just what I needed to take my mind off of things. I changed out of my pajamas and into something equally comfortable and much cooler (IMHO at the time) — a (possibly knockoff) Juicy Couture fur-lined sweatshirt that I had bought on eBay, jeans, and Uggs — put on some lip gloss, grabbed my bag (the original MAB sample, of course), and headed over to her place.

When we arrived, I surveyed the scene. It was your typical Los Angeles Saturday-night house party: self-serve bar in the kitchen, lots of clear plastic cups everywhere, and Maroon 5 blasting on the stereo. I helped myself to a weak tequila and soda and proceeded to check out every guy there. When Karen and I went outside for a cigarette, I took out my just-written description of the ultimate guy and read it from start to finish. We were both sure the person who I had described on paper did not exist. The moment we went inside, I met Gavin. I recognized him from his Myspace profile that Brie had shown me when she tried to play matchmaker the first time around. My initial reaction was that he was much hotter in real life than in his profile pic. I told Karen everything, and after a few awkward practice rounds, she pushed me—literally—into him as a conversation starter. It worked.

We hit it off immediately. I started checking off his qualities on my list. Open? Check. Funny? Check. Kind? Check. Not a jerk? Check, check, check. As we chatted the night away, talking about everything and nothing the way that you do when you're just excited to be sharing oxygen with a person, I noticed that a woman kept bopping up to us to see if Gavin wanted another drink or if he had the time. Suddenly I realized that they were on a date. Oof. I had been totally oblivious up until that point. As I excused myself, he gave me his email in case I wanted to book him and his band for the fundraiser I was helping organize. It was a legitimate reason to stay in touch—no funny business there. He was in a band, and the fundraiser that I was working on did need talent to perform—at least that's what I told myself so I didn't feel bad getting in touch.

We had a few friends in common, all of whom I contacted the next day. One mutual pal of ours happened to be his manager. As he and I were casually hanging out later, I mentioned Gavin. He asked if I was interested, and I responded by begging him to tell me everything he knew. When I finally sat down to send Gavin an email, I noticed he had found me on Myspace less than an hour before. We made a coffee date for that day. We snagged a table outside at the Alcove in Los Feliz and proceeded to drink too much coffee and smoke an entire pack of cigarettes between the two of us. As we were leaving, he confirmed what had unfolded in front of my eyes at the party, that he was in fact kind of sort of seeing someone. I played off my total devastation as best I could with a very chill, "Let me know what happens with that." One of my greatest performances of all time.

Inside I was crushed. I had already saved his phone number in my Sidekick (the hottest device pre-iPhone) with a note that said "Gavin Baby." I did my best to put the whole thing out of my head by returning to New York and the realities of running my fledgling business. Ten whole entire days later, a message popped up on my Myspace that read, "You know that thing? Well, it's not a thing anymore." We talked every day for two weeks. I flew back out to Los Angeles for the fundraiser, where I saw his band play for the first time. Afterward, we packed up his car and road-tripped to San Francisco. Insert all of your favorite romantic clichés here. We didn't care. It was love.

We lived long-distance for a year before it felt like we needed to choose between me going to Los Angeles or him moving to New York. After we weighed the options, he offered to come east. My business was just getting going, and he believed in it. He believed in me. The only place I could do what I do is New

York, and he was willing to change his entire life so that I could keep pursuing my dream.

Relocating across the country was a serious undertaking. Especially because he was doing it for me. He didn't know a ton of people. There wasn't a golden job opportunity waiting for him. It put a lot of pressure on our relationship (so did the prospect of sharing the smallest bedroom in a three-bedroom apartment). If he was going to commit to this whole new world, we both needed to feel like this was going to work for the long term.

In order to do that, we had to talk. A lot. About everything. The boring stuff, the big stuff, and everything in between. These sorts of topics of discussion are not the cutesy gushy stuff, like whether you like percale or linen sheets in the summertime. This was the nitty-gritty, like how we were going to handle our finances (we split everything right down the middle back then, just as we do now), what we wanted our lifestyle to look and feel like, and if we were aligned when it came to our hopes and dreams. No game playing. It was the first time in my life where I was able to openly talk about what I wanted and needed in a partner and from a relationship. I highly recommend going no-filter and having this sort of talk with anyone that you're thinking of getting serious with. If you're hesitant because you feel like it might scare them off, well, that might be a good thing. If they can't handle the hypotheticals, how are they going to deal with reality?

After that conversation, it was clear that Gavin and I wanted a lot of the same things out of life, but not every single thing matched up. I didn't have any doubts about the type of person Gavin was, or that he would make an amazing partner, husband, father, and friend. My hesitations came from the places where we felt the littlest bit mismatched. He loves to have music on at all times; I like silence. He likes to mess with the dimmer on the light switch till it's just right; I like them on or off. He leaves towels everywhere; I leave suitcases in the middle of the busiest walkways of the house. I admitted these concerns to my parents, and my dad, who is just about as blunt and direct as they come, laid it out for me: "Everyone is going to have warts," he said. "You just have to choose which ones you want to live with."

Fifteen years later, here we are, warts and all.

If you're in a relationship and you're not already having these conversations, it's time to get comfortable talking about what you need and to figure out how you're going to get those needs met.

BE PREPARED FOR ANYTHING . . . EVEN A PANDEMIC

As your relationship grows, your conversations will evolve too. Once Gavin and I began thinking about marriage and kids, we sat down and asked each other: What kind of parent do you want to be? How are we going to manage work and a family? We both wanted to be hands-on, involved parents, and we talked about what that would look like (from walking our kids to school to having dinner together at the table every night) and how we would each contribute. Staying in sync with our fundamentals has helped us keep it together as parents.

When COVID-19 hit New York, our time at home lifted the curtain on what it takes to keep a family running and the importance of communication in an equal partnership. Conference calls. Snack. Homeschool. Dishes. Zoom meetings. Snack. Laundry. All at once. Sunday afternoons used to be our time to divide and conquer for the week, but that morphed into catching and passing the balls as they came: Who's cooking dinner tonight? Great, I'll clean. Who is helping the older kids with schoolwork? Perfect, I'll sit with the baby. For Gavin and me, keeping our life together is a constant exercise of articulating what we have going on outside the home, what our family needs, what each of us needs, and how we're going to divide the work. When we first got together, it was more about philosophical ideals than less-than-sexy logistics, but these conversations also enabled us to adapt as we've grown our family.

Think of all these conversations as investments in your partnership. Whether it's a lover, friend, or colleague, if you want someone to be long term, don't be afraid to go deep and dig to find out what he or she is all about and what you could be together. You'll come to a greater, deeper understanding of what you're getting into and what the expectations may be. There's no way of fully anticipating what each and every phase of your life will require, but you'll always have something to talk about.

Rule #9

CREATE TWO-WAY STREETS

networking flows
both ways

Some people throw the word *networking* around like it's a bad thing, but relationships are everything in this industry. Relationships are everything in *every* industry.

Not having any insider track within the fashion industry when I first began meant that I needed to work extra hard to build my network. Fashion is notoriously cliquey. At the time, there wasn't social media. No one had leveled the playing field. The fashion world, from the shows to the parties to the right meetings with the right people, was just as exclusive and hard to get into as television makes it seem.

Networking for me involved seeking out big events, accepting every single invitation, striking up conversations with the people who seemed cool and interesting, and collecting as many business cards as possible along the way.

As time went on, I started to amass a respectable stash of contacts. My Rolodex was an analog version of LinkedIn: I took every business card I collected, stapled it to a blank index card, wrote any important details about the person on that card, and then filed it away in alphabetical order. It was sooo satisfying. I always sent a follow-up email or snail mail (mostly snail mail because email was barely a thing back then) after meeting someone for the first time. I wanted to establish connections so that if I ever needed to ask for something, it wouldn't be the first time that we were in touch. When I did need something, I kept my requests short, sweet, and specific: Could you introduce me to someone at this magazine? Do you know the best place to buy zippers in the Garment District? And I always let the person know how much I appreciated it, and if I could return the favor in any way, I would.

To me, the fundamental difference between networking and social climbing is reciprocity. It's *How can we help each other?*, not *What can you do for me?*

Connecting with people is good. Networking is expanding your community. It's about meeting new people and, through a genuine curiosity about each other, discovering what you have in common or where your interests, lives, and goals intersect. It's natural to want to help each other achieve whatever it is you're going for. You lift each other up. It doesn't have to be at the same time or in the same way. There's an understanding there and a level of support that you can count on.

Social climbing, on the other hand, is not a good look. Social climbing is meeting someone and becoming friends with her only because you think she will be able to help you someday. That's not networking. That's just using someone. And it's always very obvious from the outside exactly what is going on.

People with a lot to give, who come from positions of power, will always be viewed as networkers, not climbers—even if they share nothing and only take, take, take, all the way up—because the idea is that if they were asked for something, they would be able to come through. People starting from the bottom, with zero assets, zero connections, are often criticized as climbers, even when they share everything they have.

So when you are at the bottom of the totem pole, trying to break into an industry, and you don't bring anything tangible to the table other than yourself—when you need networking the most and don't have much to offer in return—how do you make sure you aren't just taking?

ASKING FOR A FRIEND

Getting ahead isn't about who you know; it's about who you *are*. This is true for people who luck into jobs based on who their parents are, and it's equally as true when people go out of their way to help you just because they've met you and they *like* you. How do you make sure people like you? You can't. You can only make sure that *you* like you.

Many heritage creative industries, including fashion, were never really about networking, but rather getting to the top and staying there as long as possible. That's textbook social climbing, not to mention a textbook pyramid scheme: a bunch of people toiling at the bottom with those at the top reaping all of the rewards and protecting what they have at all costs. But the internet changed everything; the pyramid is gone. There's room for many voices, and there are so many more seats at the table. That one person rolling her eyes at you doesn't matter anymore—unless that one person is you.

So always remember the people who helped you. Always remember the people who did you a favor. Always remember the people who responded to your cold calls, emails, and DMs. One way or another, it will come back to you, and you want it to be in a good way. Give back in the ways that you can. If you give back along the way, if you give back once you make it to the top, you were never a social climber.

Now, work friendships are a whole other ball game. If you are in a position of power in your business and you have a lot of friends in your industry, chances are that some of those friendships won't stick around if you change careers (or if you lose your position of power). If this is the case, you might ask yourself: Could you be subconsciously collecting friends based on what people can do for you rather than any genuine feelings of friendship?

Your professional contacts can easily become your closest friends. Your friends can become your most trusted collaborators and colleagues. A relationship can vacillate between the two. But as long as the connection is authentic, as long as there's a true friendship base, it shouldn't get awkward.

FOR YEARS, I was in almost-daily contact with an editor at one of the fashion-trade publications. I would send her anything newsy that I thought she would be interested in, even if it wasn't just my brand. We could talk shop about business trends, and I was top of mind for her if she had a story where I was a good fit. She was never that in love with her job, so, when she wanted to make a switch, I was there for her as a sounding board and kept my ears open for any opportunities that had real potential. She eventually landed an amazing corporate job in a different industry, but it had zero overlap with my work. The nature of our relationship changed. How could it not? In her new role, we just didn't have as many reasons to connect as often as we once did. But that's okay—our relationship evolved, and we will always be friends, even if we don't have our daily industry chats.

On the other hand, I have another close friend, an editor who covered the accessories market at a respected magazine, who lost her job when her magazine closed the print edition to go 100 percent digital. She started looking for a new job right away, but no one was hiring. After a few weeks, she noticed that a few of her friends stopped replying to her texts. Her emails went unanswered. She wasn't invited to go to SoulCycle on Saturday mornings. What did these disappearing friends all have in common? They were all publicists with accessory brands as major clients. Was there a happy ending? A year later, she got a much bigger editorial job at a more important media outlet, and, within twenty-four hours, those publicist friends had sent texts, flowers, and Saturday SoulCycle invites. Losing a job is hard. Losing your friends along with it makes it even harder. My friend was thrilled to have her amazing new role, but she has never been the same when it comes to friendships. They really broke her heart.

So how do you make sure that your friends-with-work-benefits won't lead to heartbreak, either for you or for them? Yep, you guessed it: reciprocity. You can do a check-in by considering the following questions:

How does this person show up in your day-to-day life? How do you show up in theirs?

Do they check in with you regularly, or only when they need something? When do you check in with them?

Is your relationship collaborative or competitive?

Do you only talk about your work? Do you only talk about their work?

Good friends are good friends, whether you work together or not. Business or personal, the healthiest, best relationships are mutually beneficial. In order to keep your connections positively charged, make sure that you're not the only person getting something out of them. If you're asking for favors, intro-ductions, or help, be prepared to offer the same in return. It doesn't have to be an exact exchange of the same sort of help at that very moment in time. It might turn into an IOU. That's okay. You might ask for an introduction and be able to give an intro-duction, but maybe instead your friend will call on you down the line to help her work through an issue or provide informa-tion about a resource that you have access to. Whatever it is, be ready and willing to help however you can.

Rule #10

CHANGE THINGS UP

change is

inevitable

and enviable

I t's really easy to become attached to an idea. You spend all this time trying to come up with the perfect version of whatever something may be — it could be as small as your basic morning beauty routine or something with much higher stakes, like a product or service — so once you've figured it out, you want it to stay that way. You've already done the hard part of creating it and getting it just right, so why change?

While it's great to have an amazing idea, you don't want that to be the end of the road. How can that be it? You want your idea to come to life, then grow, expand, and build on itself. If you refuse or resist changing, then you and your idea will be left behind.

The MAB really took on a life of its own. I didn't make another bag style for two years. People were hungry for that bag. And I wanted to give the people what they wanted.

Things were going along swimmingly until Satine decided they were going to close the showroom. For a designer, the closing of a showroom was like the severing of a lifeline to the outside world of buyers and stores. It was my portal to selling bags. Direct-to-consumer selling was not yet a thing and social media was nothing like it is today, so brands relied on their sales reps to tell them everything that the buyers were extremely into and excited about or completely over and never wanted to see ever again. Without a showroom, sales would at best plateau, at worst plummet. Things were about to change. I crossed my fingers and hoped it was for the best.

ALWAYS ROOM FOR IMPROVEMENT

In the entire industry, there were only two showrooms where I really wanted to be. It wasn't hard to get meetings with the sales reps. People knew my name, and good salespeople follow up on every potential lead. No one wants to make the mistake of turning the next big thing away. But getting into the right showroom, where they have the right contacts and a dynamic roster of brands, is like lifting the couch on moving day and finding the single missing piece of the jigsaw puzzle that you started last summer, finally giving you a chance for closure: it makes you feel things are going to go your way.

I called and made an appointment to meet with the indie-bag-queen-maker of the moment, Cynthia O'Connor. Accessories brands were popping up left and right, and every brand she took on caught fire. I had heard she was hard-core—from the way she ran her business to the way she gave feedback—and even though I was slightly intimidated, I had a hit bag. That had to be worth something.

The receptionist greeted me and led me past shelves and racks of next season's accessories from all of the brands and designers that were huge at the time. She dropped me off in their glass-walled conference room where I was to wait.

There wasn't much small talk. Just hi, hello, nice to meet you, thanks for coming. But once the general pleasantries were out of the way, Cynthia got right down to business and proceeded to tear the MAB apart. She critiqued everything, from the materials and the proportions to the finishing and quality—she went off on all of the shortcomings of my choice to use brass hardware for a solid ten minutes (it ages, dulls, and shows spots unless you polish it all the time). I can't even tell you everything that she said because I only remember that she hated everything about it.

By the time she was finished, I was shocked she had taken the meeting at all. She was launching all the biggest independent handbag lines at the time, and there I was with my four little handbag styles. When she told me to come back with a fixed bag and a better plan, I was floored. I really didn't know what to say.

In the span of fifteen minutes, I had gone from being confident and proud to flat-out humbled. Up until that meeting, I thought I was in pretty good shape. But according to her, I had so much work to do.

After hearing only good things and reading only love letters about the MAB for ages, to have someone tell me everything that was wrong with it took me by surprise. I had been prepared for her to ask me about what else I had in production and who my die-hard fans were. I loved the MAB and the huge wave of momentum that had carried me to this point in my career. I wasn't expecting her to pick apart my little bag baby stitch by stitch. Change can be scary. It was an understatement to say that the notion of changing something that I knew was working in the market and that I knew how to produce was daunting. In some ways I felt like I had just hit my stride, and now she was telling me that if I ever wanted to make something real happen, I was going to have to do things differently.

She really lit a fire under my ass.

I could have left her office in a huff and convinced myself that what I had was working and that I knew my customers better. But I wanted a forever brand. And if I was going to achieve that, things were going to have to change, not only in respect to the bag, but in respect to the business and my way of doing things as a whole. When I designed the bag, I wanted something that looked good, did its job, and made people happy when they wore it.

The callouts she made were on point. Could the bag be better? Yes, there is always room for improvement. And the types of changes she was telling me to make might have seemed superficial — a more expensive buckle here or a lining with a nicer feel — but making these changes impacted the foundation of my brand. I didn't want to be a one-hit wonder and then disappear into obscurity. I wanted to build a lasting business, and to do that, I needed to dial in the details so that my bags could go the distance.

I implemented everything that she said in a week. Whether or not she decided to take me on, I knew that I had completely upped my game. I found better fabrics and leathers at the same price. I broke down the supply-chain issues that were causing spotty hardware quality and restructured everything to be way more efficient. At this point, it was just me, an intern, and Uri on speed dial, so while these things sound really big, it was more a matter of me trying to do things a different way. I stayed up night after night going over every little detail of our design, production, and business plans to make sure that we were in fact doing things as professionally and profitably as possible. Everything was just better. I was ready to go back.

Two weeks later, when I called to schedule the follow-up appointment, her assistant put me on hold. Cynthia picked up the phone. "I really didn't think you'd be back," she said. Apparently, there were plenty of designers who didn't want to hear what she had to say and who had gone on their way after meeting with her. But there I was.

This time, our meeting went much differently. She looked over the bag for a long time. She picked it up, unzipped it, and began to scrutinize every crook and every corner. I was shaking. I had already convinced myself that her showroom was the absolute best and the only place I wanted to be. I wasn't prepared for her to say no, but I knew it was a real possibility. After several minutes of inspection, she put the bag down. "Not bad," she said. "This is a real improvement. I still see some things that need to get fixed—and you have to figure out how to do that quickly—but I am willing to take you on." If I hadn't been trying to play it cool, I would have done a backflip right then and there in the conference room.

This was the proof she needed that I was serious about building a brand, not just selling a bag. Our meeting was the first time in my career that someone gave me straightforward, clear criticism and direction. I had experienced acceptance and rejection, but no one had invested the energy to be constructive. She didn't sugarcoat a thing. Did I have to listen to her? No. I could have walked away and taken meetings at every other showroom in New York. My bag was definitely popular enough at that point to help me get a foot in the door. But if I was going to ignore everything she had to say and just keep doing things the way that I had been doing them, what was the point of that meeting at all?

I respected her and her accomplishments. She knew what she was doing, and the brands she launched succeeded. She might have been a hard-ass, but no one else was taking the time to talk to me about the consistency and quality of my hardware. That type of insight truly improved the quality of my bags and allowed me to keep building. If she was paying that much attention, it must have meant that she cared. Or if she didn't care, at least she saw the potential for my brand to grow. She certainly didn't seem like the type to take meetings for fun. It's one thing to give someone casual feedback. It's another thing to invest real energy into helping someone shape her vision into success. Whether or not you take someone's advice determines whether or not that person will keep doling it out. If Cynthia was going to take me on, it had to be worth her time.

No matter how often we hear "change is good," it doesn't make change any less scary. Change means things are going to be different, and people often automatically assume that *different* means *worse*. An opportunity to try something a different way is an opportunity for growth. Doing away with the preconceived notion that things have to be handled in a particular manner is freedom. If someone you admire, someone you believe truly knows what she is talking about, makes a few suggestions of ways to evolve what you're creating, why not give it a shot?

When the opportunity comes along for improvement, it's a sign you're on the right track. You're going somewhere.

Rule #11

SKIP THE SHORTCUTS

no one is

timing you

T here are shortcuts in life, but they are never what you want them to be. Take a long, arduous, and annoying thing and turn it into something quick and easy? Who wouldn't love that? My husband says I think about this quite often and lovingly calls it "Becky Math"—I might try really hard to stretch a budget out, but the math just doesn't add up the way I want it to, or I might somehow calculate that I have earned more parent points than him, though I am always biased in my favor.

The reality is that shortcuts and cutting corners have never paid off for me. Not once. There have been times that I've had to get a website up quickly and we've used templates and plug-ins to speed up the process, and of course we eventually have had to rebuild them. I've pulled favors for introductions to executives and then realized the person whose help would be the most valuable would be someone who was critically involved in the business's day-to-day. Even when someone tells me about a back road to avoid traffic, I'm the one who gets trapped behind a garbage truck for an hour and winds up at a dead end in the woods. Same goes for trying to take the shortest or earlier flight home so I can rush back to my kids—you guessed it, there's always a delay or a canceled flight. This has happened more times than I can count. Just me and a bad airport salad hanging out.

THE MASH-UP FROM HELL

Around 2007, we decided to begin producing our bags overseas. Through a long chain of business associates and work colleagues, we finally hit what we thought was the jackpot: a factory in China that was responsible for producing Kate Spade bags. Boom. Done. What could be better than having the same production as one of the most popular lines in the world? I thought we were set.

Everything seemed to be going along swimmingly. Business was good. Our retail presence was growing. Orders were being fulfilled on time. We were cruising right along. Then one day I was surfing PurseForum, where I liked to spend as much time as possible reading what all the shoppers and fans had to say. I came across a post about one of my bags. I clicked. When the post opened, I saw what looked like a classic Rebecca Minkoff bag on the outside, but on the inside, it was finished with Kate Spade hardware.

My. Jaw. Dropped.

A comment with the post read: "What's a hybrid of Kate Spade and Rebecca Minkoff?"

Two words: Kabecca Spankoff.

I know, I know. It's hilarious. But truthfully, I can barely laugh about it now. Just barely.

To say I was mortified was an understatement. If the coffin emoji had existed at the time, it would have been perfect. I wanted to crawl under a rock and hide for the rest of my life. I thought my business was over. Something like this could completely ruin you. I prayed that this wouldn't be the end of Rebecca Minkoff.

Now, I knew quality control was a thing. I just naively thought that we could skip over that part of the process, since it seemed unnecessary when we were working with such a major factory and it would definitely slow down the production of our bags. We also didn't think it was a great way to spend the money that we had at the time. Every hire meant that we had to be bigger and make more money, and all of our cash was going into production. But finding a reputable factory with such high-profile accounts felt like a safe way around this. I didn't really think twice about it. What could go wrong?

Every established part of a process is a part of the process for a reason. That's not to say that you have to do things exactly the way they have been done before. But coming up with innovative processes is very different than skipping processes to save time and money, especially as a global brand.

Cutting corners because you think it's going to get you results easier, faster, or cheaper rarely works out. If I had just gotten on a plane and gone to China, if I had asked them to send us a sample bag, if I had asked them to email us a photo, this would have never happened. By assuming I could cut corners by eliminating an essential part of the production process because of time or financials, I really screwed myself. If we had done quality control instead of skipping that part of the process entirely, Kabecca Spankoff would have never seen the light of day. But instead, here she was all over the internet, looking like a hot, mislabeled, poorly studded mess.

I didn't know what to do.

It was obviously a huge mistake. Luckily it was so big and so ridiculously bad that people thought it was hilarious.

Looking at the situation, I realized I had two options: I could go in the direction of OMG-I-am-so-sorry-this-is-the-worst and call attention to the colossal mistakes that I had made, or I could somehow miraculously play it off as a goof and hopefully get people laughing with me, not at me.

I typed a reply to the post: "Congrats! You found this bag. We'll ship you not only a replacement, but a special new bag too!" I crossed my fingers and waited.

It created a feeding frenzy.

Suddenly people wanted these crazy, messed-up bags more than any other bags we were making.

I wish this were where the story ended. But no, there's more.

Things were looking sunny on the community side, but we had the factory to deal with. When we finally got in touch and had a proper freak-out, they agreed to remake the bags free of charge. They said they were so sorry and that they had found the source of the confusion. They said something like this would never, ever, ever happen again. We had their word.

Was this the point where we hired a quality-control person? Nope. Did we send someone to China? We didn't do that either. Why? We thought that if we made the phone calls and had talked to the people in charge, that should be good enough. We didn't need to worry about hiring someone right then and there. We could deal with that later.

I guess I really needed to learn this lesson the hard way be-cause you might imagine what happened next.

Round two of Kabecca Spankoff purses were shipped to de-partment stores, boutiques, and individuals—some of whom were supposed to be receiving replacements for the first Ka-becca Spankoff bags they had found.

I died.

And then I hired someone to do quality control.

There are no shortcuts when it comes to doing what needs to be done. There are no shortcuts for the 168-hour weeks that you will put in. There's no way around the sacrifices that you have to make, whether it's not having a social life or spending your money on buttons instead of a brunch. You will always have to put your head down and do the work, whether it's making it happen the first time around or working twice as hard and spending twice as much money to fix a mistake.

Choosing to take shortcuts can actually rob you of valuable experience. You can know Point A, and you can know Point B, but if you have no idea of what goes into getting from one to the other, you'll never be able to get there on your own or show another person the way. As an entrepreneur and a designer, it has helped that I know how to sew, have put in the grunt work to source fabric and hardware, have dealt with all levels of production, and have done almost every job that we hire someone to do at my company. That's certainly not to say that I was the best at every aspect of this business—the whole goal is to get to a place where you can hire the people to do the jobs you aren't that good at, or don't like, so they can do them better than you would do them yourself.

Good things take time.

Rule #12

PLAY THE WILD CARD

go on and

take the risk

Y ou never know when something is going to hit. There are many ways that you can feel aligned with your community and customer. I've spent years of my life on purse blogs, in forums, and listening to our community in person and on social media. You can also have a really keen sense of the trends and what may come next. And you might be right about it, but there's no way of knowing whether or not your interpretation of that new mood is going to be the one that resonates with the crowd.

Sometimes life deals you a wild card.

JUST SAY YES

In 2003, I was in Los Angeles when my dad called. He asked if he could give his friend's son my number. It sounded like a setup, but it wasn't. Apparently, the son was making a reality television show, and they wanted to shoot an episode at a fashion event. I said sure, have him give me a call. When this total stranger and I eventually connected, he explained it was a small cast of just a few friends from Orange County, and they were going to drive up to attend my fashion event.

My initial reaction was that this sounded like a dumb show. Why were they filming these kids that no one had ever heard of and putting them on TV? But hey, I was just a young designer having a fashion show for my clothing collection at an art gallery in Downtown LA when it was still cool-adjacent. Who was I to turn down an opportunity to be on television? I said yes. If a TV crew wanted to come in and film some nobodies watching my fashion show, that was fine by me. It was real any-exposure-is-good-exposure thinking. I didn't have press clawing over each other to get in the door. I pretended to check my seating chart, and it looked like, yes, it would be possible to get a few seats in the front row. Done and done.

When show day came, I was fully consumed prepping the models backstage. The cast and crew showed up just before the lights went down on the makeshift catwalk. The music kicked in, and I sent models out to strut their stuff. They walked in a square, dressed in a lot of asymmetrical jerseys, while the baby-faced blonde real-people actors talked about how skinny is too skinny. It was a perfect snapshot in time. It turned out to be a little show called *Laguna Beach*. And everyone went absolutely wild for it.

In 2009, MTV started airing reruns of *Laguna Beach*, including the episode that was shot at my fashion show. When it re-aired, my phone started ringing off the hook. Buyers were calling and saying, "Why didn't you tell me this was happening?" and "How could you bring back apparel and not say anything?" The show was not some groundbreaking, innovative directional collection that was going to change the future of fashion. There was a black halter top, a peach jersey miniskirt, a pink low-rise pantsuit, and so many other very 2003 things that I would never be caught wearing now. But people said they wanted clothing, so of course I wanted to give it to them. (Just not the stretchy red one-shouldered shirt that they had just seen on an old TV show.)

Since the interest was there, I wanted to act fast. People are fickle. I went into my closet and pulled out every piece I loved. I hauled it all to work and, together with the small team I had at the time, evaluated each item one by one. For each piece, I asked myself, *Why do you love this?* I was picking pieces that had a story behind them or that had an incredible detail, color, pattern, print, or texture. I was picking things that made me feel confident when I threw them on even on days when I didn't want to get out of bed. I wanted to make the kind of clothing that you could wear every day but that wasn't basic.

Then the conversation shifted. Guesses about the market, concern for the bottom line, and the general feeling of "Are we sure about this?" redirected the creative conversation into a technical, number-crunchy, formulaic exercise: "Will it sell?" had become the way we evaluated the concepts and styles. It was missing the heart that I felt like I always brought to design—it was my first love—but maybe this was what needed to happen in order to make it work this time around.

BE TRUE TO YOUR BRAND

People were excited about the clothing. We had brought it to market in weeks instead of months, and it showed. It existed, but it wasn't built on a solid foundation. If you run a small business, remember that you are in control of your choices and actions. You have the ability to be nimble, and also to do things at your own pace, thoughtfully and carefully. In the heat of the moment, it's easy to forget that. Our handbag business was big, and it was operating on that level. Because we felt the pressure to do the clothing line in the same way that we were doing our bags, we didn't take the time to think it through and set it up correctly.

The collection wound up being more of what I thought people wanted from me and less of what I wanted for myself. To say it was a huge failure sounds harsh, so I'll just say it was a big failure to soften the blow. Sad but true. It was only ten pieces, but the collection had lost any semblance of direction or inspiration. I was just trying to check all the boxes of what I thought the collection needed to be, instead of putting my creative energy into the process.

To a certain extent, your audience wants what they want, but they also want what you want to give them. Deciding to do it your way doesn't mean that you're not listening to the customer. If you're not going to put your spin on it, they might as well make it themselves. They are coming to you for a reason.

I just had to keep trying. It all felt so unpredictable, but I wasn't going to give up so fast. After the first season, Ilaria (who had helped launch the MAB) and I started talking about the collection in a more fun, conceptual way. We shared ideas, mood boards, samples, and themes. She helped unify and focus it. Having a partner to bounce ideas off of changed the trajectory of the line completely. It went from "What will sell?" to "Wouldn't it be amazing if . . ." It was the work that needed to be done to give the apparel side of the business a real point of view and purpose: It should not be ten random things that I pulled from my closet. It should be the uniform of the girl who ruled the world from her MAB. Enter in flirty twist-front dresses, silk button-downs, skinny jeans, and the shrunken leather jackets that have become staples in my line. Finally, I was making clothing for the Downtown Romantic.

GO AT YOUR OWN PACE

The next few years, the work was creatively satisfying, but the business was up and down. There were collections that the press and people flipped out over, that received so much attention and loads of positive coverage, but that didn't sell.

When it came time to actually buy what we had sent down the runway, it seemed like our Downtown Romantic was not interested. She had seen it in the magazines and all over the internet months before, so when it hit shops, she was over it. We were doing things just like everybody else in the industry: design and produce a collection, spend tons of money to do a runway show with all the big names at New York Fashion Week, and then cross our fingers in hopes that the magazines would cover it and the buyers would love it.

We were putting in hundreds of thousands of dollars to create billions of media impressions for clothing that people couldn't have for another six to nine months. Plus—and this is why so many luxury brands resisted having their looks appear online in the early days—before our orders were even shipped, I would see knockoffs pop up at all the fast-fashion shops for a fraction of the price. No wonder our girl didn't want it from us. She was getting it cheaper and faster from somewhere else. The lag time between showing the collection and shopping the collection was totally killing us.

How did we get here? Why were we doing this? It would have made more sense if Fashion Week were shrouded in secrecy, with every image and review embargoed until the clothing was ready to hit the stores, but it was not.

Why did we feel this pressure to do it this way, the way that everyone else was doing it? Why did we have to show, sell, and ship at the same time as everyone else? I felt this pressure to be taken seriously by the fashion world, and I believed that in order to do that, I had to do things just like everyone else was doing them. But why?

There was no playbook. I didn't have to do anything I didn't want to do. Did our girl even care about the shows? It's not like she was invited. It seemed like all she wanted to do was be able to buy the cute dress she saw on Instagram as soon as possible. How were we going to figure out a different way? It was time.

When things go awry, it's natural to start asking yourself why things are the way things are. This line of questioning can be really helpful when you're trying to learn from your past experiences and grow from them. "Why" questions are often stuck in the past, so they can keep you stuck there too. "How" questions are the type of questions that will help push you toward solutions. Asking why things are the way they are might land you on an explanation, but asking how you are going to get to where you want to go is what will move you forward.

If we were going to keep the clothing line going, we needed to try something completely new and different.

For our price point and category, it had clearly stopped making sense for us to have a big reveal. Why not just show people what they could have right then and there instead of what they might want in six months? Enter the See Buy Wear fashion show, a celebration of the current season where everything we sent down the runway would be ready to take home. As revolutionary as it felt, it also just sounded logical.

For our first show, we got the collection ready, invited buyers in for their appointments, took orders, and then produced the pieces that sold. Six months later, we put on the show, and people were able to buy what they had just seen and wear it right when they wanted to.

While everyone was showing cozy cashmere and tweed for Fall/Winter, we were sending models down the runway in full fuchsia, royal blue, and neon yellow just in time for Spring/Summer. I was used to sticking out at this point. And it was a good thing. Deciding to be in real time meant that all of the exposure, all of the eyeballs, all of the marketing, and all of the social chatter actually started driving sales. There was no way of knowing if it was going to work out for sure, but we took a chance, played the wild card, and won.

Rule #13

BE THERE FOR IT

make yourself

available

P laying hard to get is overrated. The idea that exclusivity and desirability have to go hand in hand has been around for ages. If it feels like an old way of thinking, that's because it is. To some extent, it's baked into our brains to look outward for what we don't have instead of focusing on what we do have. The rarer and more special something seems, or the more difficult something is to get your hands on, the more you feel like you absolutely have to have it at all costs and you become determined to make it yours.

But as a designer and from a brand point of view, there is another option: get your stuff into as many people's hands as possible. Instead of being the carrot dangling out there in space all alone, hoping that someone will find you tempting, cut yourself loose and go make friends with the bunnies that you know for a fact are obsessed with you. Inclusivity is the new exclusivity.

Everyone likes to say that they were there when [insert amazingly meaningful event of personal or cultural importance here].

But to really be there for anything, you have to actually make an effort.

DOWN BUT NOT OUT

One of the most important things that happened at the beginning of the 2008 recession was a conversation with one of our major retailers about our price point. They said, "You did really well, and we want to renew your contract, but if you keep your pricing as high as it is, we won't be able to put you on the floor. But here's the thing: you can't lower the quality, or people will notice and no one will want you."

Cool. Same bag. Sell it for less. Got it. Makes total sense on some other planet.

It would be very difficult to lower our prices. Without touching the materials we were using, the production we had established and trusted, or any of the other aspects that went into creating our bags, we would basically be selling the same exact bag but for less money, which meant making less money. We weren't going to make cheaper bags, but we needed to figure out how to charge less for them.

Of course, this was not ideal for a million reasons. I had worked really hard to establish the brand and the bag as being a good value for the price. It's not like that price came out of thin air. It was definitely on par with what other brands at the same level were charging. The sweet spot for an It Bag back then was around $500, and that's what we charged. Compared to super high-end luxury brands, it was on the low end of what people were spending on designer bags. On the other hand, it was an of-the-moment bag that was made to be a tried-and-true go-to, so it was easy to justify the price tag knowing that you were going to use it every single day. We'd used formulas to arrive at that price point. Taking into account the cost of our raw goods, the caliber of the makers and factories that we worked with, and all of the other arms of the business that touched the making of the bag from start to finish, we felt like we had priced it fairly. But if we wanted to stay with our retail partners, we needed to make the change. They hadn't given us an option; they were telling us what to do.

This decision would have long-range implications too. Once we changed the price point for one retailer, that meant we were changing our prices, period. We would need to adjust the prices on our e-commerce site and across the board for all of the shops, boutiques, and department stores. Would we look like we were in trouble, desperate to make a sale? Would it seem like we had fallen out of fashion and were suddenly discounting ourselves?

It was easy to freak out, but I tried to find the upside. One thing that dropping our prices would mean was that our bags would become more accessible. But that could be good or bad depending on whom you asked. Those who thought going lower was a good thing really embraced the idea that a more approachable price would make the bag attainable for more people—which meant that we would sell more of them. Those who said changing our price point was going to hurt us wanted to hold on to the benefits that come with being an aspirational brand. I'll admit it: there is a part of me—it's called my ego, and I know it very well—that wanted to be part of that glossy designer scene. But when it came down to it, the price of my bags wasn't the key to that kingdom. The more and more I thought about it, the more I felt like what was important was to meet our girl where she was: trying to get a stylish, well-made bag for a good price that made her feel good when she walked out the door. Not to mention we were in a recession. So we decided to cut our prices. After a lot of back-and-forth, and a lot of fear about how this would affect the future of the brand, it seemed like being there for our girl now was just the right thing to do.

So then what? Our new bags hit, and the price was lowered. I got my first gray hair due to stressing over this. We waited for our sales to increase (cue the drumroll . . .), and nothing happened. Nada. Sales stayed the same, and reverting to our original price point with a *JK!* or a *Not!* was not an option. We pulled up our big-girl pants and settled in. Then, three long months later, it hit—and it hit big. Like 548 percent big. We could not keep up. We didn't see a huge jump in profits, but our bags were suddenly being worn by more people in more places across the country than ever before. In the short term it felt the choice was going to be a setback, but the big picture showed us it was a huge step in the right direction for the company as a whole.

MEET HER WHERE SHE IS

The true gain of reducing our prices was the fact that we had connected even more with our girl. You know how going through something intense with someone brings you closer together? It felt like that. It was like we had weathered the blows that the recession dealt us and come out stronger together on the other side. If we were friends before, we were besties now. With our bags being more accessible, we were able to show up for her in new and different ways.

At first, we were the cool bag that our girl scrimped and saved for; she was willing to trade dinner out with friends for Cup O'Noodles on the couch if it meant that she could put the extra cash toward her purchase. We had been the once-a-year fashion indulgence that she allowed herself. Then, I began hearing these very personal, very real stories of the role that our bags were playing in people's lives. I would be at a trunk show and someone would come up to me and introduce herself, and then she'd start her story by saying, "I have to tell you, my first Rebecca Minkoff was when . . ." What followed was always something about one of the bags from the collection being the bag that she bought for her job interview, the purse that she treated herself to as a birthday present, or the gift that her girl-friends had all chipped in on. I hadn't really thought about our bags in that way before. If we were able to be there for all of the important moments in our girl's life, and if having a bag that she loved made her feel like she was being her best self and living her best life, then that was way more important to me than be-ing part of a higher price range.

Understanding that there was an emotional connection to our brand only motivated me to be there for more moments in our girl's life. If she wanted me to be there with her for her first interview, I was going to be there, and I was going to give her a bag that fit her computer. If she needed me to go away with her for the weekend with her new boyfriend, I was going to make her an overnight bag that fit all her dresses and heels and that could also fit in the overhead rack on the Long Island Rail Road. Shit. If she wanted me to go to her wedding, I was going to make her a jewel-shaped clutch that would fit her lipstick, breath mints, and a few safety pins. Now when we design our bags, we think of how we can fit into our girl's lifestyle and where we can be there for her along the way.

I wasn't above it all. I was there for it. I was exactly where I had always wanted to be.

Rule #14

UNFOLLOW

break from
the pack and go
your own way

I f you want the same old things, do things the same old way. When you get up in the morning and go about your routine, there are no surprises. That's the thing about routines. You know what's coming. People stay comfortable in their routines for years, even decades. However, if you're trying to bring something unique into this world, you're going to need to find an equally unique way of doing it.

When I started working with Cynthia and the team in her showroom, I definitely felt more established, but I still felt like the ground could fall out from underneath me anytime. I don't think I've ever felt truly secure in my career. Life is crazy. Weird shit happens. Nobody can predict the future.

Some people are pure optimists and feel like everything is always going to be sunshine and rainbows. I'm more of a feet-on-the-ground realist with a reasonable amount of positivity sprinkled on top: it would be nice if everything could be sunshine and rainbows all the time, but there's always a chance of rain, because we aren't the boss of the weather. (Perhaps we should take this opportunity to start manufacturing really chic umbrellas.)

So, even though working with Cynthia made me feel like I had advanced in my career, I didn't feel like I had made it. But it was a big step forward, and it felt really good to know that I wasn't the only one taking my business seriously anymore.

THE RIGHT DIRECTION

The showroom had a very specific way of working. Cynthia gave all of her clients a handbook to read and then asked them to sign paperwork acknowledging that they had read, understood, and would abide by everything in it. If you didn't follow her methodology, you were out. If she called with criticisms or suggestions and you ignored her feedback, you were out. If you deviated at all from the channels of communication with her sales team, you were out. I was her soldier, and whatever she said, I would do it.

For press—and pretty much everything else—I was on my own. All my money was going to the showroom, and I couldn't afford to hire a fancy publicist too. Looking back, I'm not even sure how much it would have helped. It definitely felt like there was an elite fashion clique and that I was not part of it. The same designers seemed to be profiled and featured again and again and again. No matter what I did, how well my bags were selling, or which celebrities and influencers were fans, I couldn't get any of the editors at the glossy fashion magazines interested in the brand or me as a designer or business owner. After living and working in New York for nearly twenty years now, I have made many good friends in the industry, but back then, I felt like I was not cool enough or connected enough or successful enough or rich enough to run in those circles.

Once I accepted that I was an outsider, it really freed me up to do whatever I wanted, however I wanted to do it. I didn't need to fit into anyone's mold, and neither did my business. But in order for people to want the bags, people needed to know the bags existed. I needed to come up with a new way to make this happen, since I didn't have access to doing it the way everyone else did.

In school they teach us that two plus two equals four. Over and over again. We've all heard it a trillion times. When you hear or see an equation repeatedly, it's easy to fall into thinking that it is the one and only way to get the outcome you're going for. But, hey, one plus three also equals four, and two and a half plus one and a half equals four as well. No matter how simple and how obvious the solution may seem, remember there are many ways to get there.

FIRST, YOU MUST GIVE IT AWAY

In between launching The Shirt and coming out with the MAB, I had learned the power of celebrity placement. It wasn't a new concept: the idea of using well-known people to endorse products goes way back to ancient times, when makers would tout their wares to the public once they were used by the local royals—pharaohs, caesars, anyone with a gold crown. The logic has forever been the same: if it's good enough for the queen, it's good enough for all you regular people too.

Gifting became a huge part of how I operated and grew the brand. Marketers had just started organizing gifting suites: they would invite a bunch of companies to set up booths and give their wares away to celebrities. The term *celebrity* was used very loosely, covering everyone from A-listers in their "undercover" black baseball caps to Z-listers, who usually cruised around with an entourage that included a tiny dog and multiple assistants. I had decided to do one at a hotel on Central Park South, and I roped Ilaria in for the day. After being there for hours, I took a bathroom break. The second I got back, Ilaria said, "Lindsay Lohan was just here, and I ran her out a bag!" I hauled ass down to the front of the hotel, and there was Lindsay Lohan, at her peak of fame and coolness, holding the MAB. The paparazzi were going nuts. I knew that if a celebrity was photographed with the bag and that image ran in the weeklies, that bag would sell. The orders would pour in. This was a really big deal.

In those days, part of Cynthia's sales philosophy was that a label needed to have a presence in five hundred specialty stores in order to have the brand awareness needed to succeed in a department store. The idea was that in order to really have brand recognition, enough to stop people in their tracks while they are shopping for Lovely by Sarah Jessica Parker and a new pair of Spanx, shoppers would have needed to see you repeatedly in other places. You needed to feel familiar to them. People don't go to department stores to discover new things; they go to have a social shopping experience where there's something for everyone. No one is saying, "Oh, what's this new brand I have never heard of?" They appreciate having so many well-known brands under one roof. We were nowhere near five hundred specialty stores when the (insert famous department store here) came calling, but we weren't going to turn them down.

That order was huge: over three hundred bags. It felt like the moment I had been waiting for. I was so proud to finally get into a department store, and I envisioned the bags selling like hotcakes. When you're first starting out, big retailers treat you like a sweet, delicate, darling little bird; they want to listen to you sing and pet you all the time. Don't have enough money in the budget to pay to be included in their ads or mailers? No worries! "We're having a catalog shoot," they tell you, "that would normally cost your company $40,000 to be featured in, but we'll waive the fee because we would love to introduce you to our audience. They're going to adore you, just like we do." Then, once you're in, things change. One day you could get an email order for 2,500 bags, but they reserve the right to cancel the order at any time, and if they do take the 2,500 bags, they could charge you back for any that don't sell. All of this is considered completely normal and the cost of doing business. Brands believe they have to go along with it because these retailers have incredible reach (they still do, to this day). The whole experience is like a super-intense relationship that can be really fun and flashy but that sometimes makes you wonder if you're being taken advantage of (because it often feels like you are). How do I know? Well, the bags didn't sell. The Big Famous Department Store returned almost all of them. Yes. Nearly three hundred bags arrived right back at my tiny apartment door.

TALK A LOT OF SHOP

Sample sales were just becoming a thing at the time. They were fun for shoppers but not that cool for brands. It was more of a utility for designers and showrooms to make a little extra cash while they cleaned out their storage, unloading all the junk from past seasons, the damaged goods, and the crusty samples that had been long forgotten. If you took your time, focused, and dug around, you could find a gem. People loved them because the prices were so incredibly low. It wasn't until designers started doing sample sales to get rid of actual stock—not just the castoffs—that it caught on as an opportunity to make real revenue. I hadn't done one before because I had never had enough extra merch lying around. Now that I had an apartment full of cardboard boxes that were full of bags from said "partner" above, I figured we might as well give it a shot. I organized the whole thing in just a few days, got it listed on the internet in a couple of places, and priced the bags to move.

The day of the sale, people started lining up at 6:00 a.m. By the time we opened the doors at 9:00 a.m., there was a line down the block. Every bag was gone by the end of the day, but that wasn't even the best part. I had put on fashion shows before, gone to countless editor meet-and-greets, and tried to connect with as many professionals in the business as possible, but the sample sale was the first time I had the opportunity to hang with my customers. The energy in the tiny little living room, filled with wall-to-wall bags and frenzied shoppers, was totally electric. I got to eavesdrop on what people were saying—the good, the bad, and the ugly. There was huge value in meeting our customers. It filled me up to see people go gaga for these bags that I had made. This was much more fun than letting the bags languish on some department-store shelf.

Even if it wasn't the cool thing to do, or even if it made me look too accessible, I didn't care. I just wanted people to be able to buy a bag that they loved so that I could support myself and my growing team and keep doing what I loved. The bags weren't free, but by cutting out the cluttered distribution situation in the middle, I could offer them at a more accessible price point. It might not be Fifth Avenue. It was definitely not polished and poised. But it was busy and fun. I didn't need to worry what anybody besides our shoppers thought. It worked for me and our community, and that's what mattered most.

Soon after that, we started doing sample sales twice a year. They became an amazing way to get the bags into people's hands directly, but they also worked as free (yet priceless) focus groups for me to see what people were into in a real way. Getting criticism from your peers or sales team is one thing—it's often constructive and delivered in a soft, thoughtful way that makes taking the input to heart feel very optional. It's another thing entirely to overhear an overly caffeinated woman carrying a dozen bags talk about how obsessed she is. Or to have a table full of one particular style left untouched the entire day. You really get an honest read on what's working and what isn't.

My dear friend Patrick summed it up perfectly: "When you followed your own path, you won. When you tried to follow others, you didn't." Sometimes you just need a reminder that you pave your own path. Consciously walking your own path is a daily choice, and it's often when we're staring into the distance that it can feel tempting to seek out another person's tracks. While there's no map, embracing your originality and learning from others aren't mutually exclusive. It's simply about context. Look to others for inspiration rather than direction. Learn what you can from those you admire; then make it yours.

There is only one you. (Do I sound like a mom right now? I feel like I sound like a mom for sure.) No one will ever be able to do what you do exactly the way that you do it, so take advantage of that. You're the captain of your own ship, even if it doesn't feel that way sometimes.

Don't be afraid to break from the pack. If something's not working, try doing it a different way. When you feel like you have something unique to say or something special to offer the world, don't feel like you have to go about doing things exactly the same way they have been done before. It's great to know the rules, but you don't have to follow them. It's a choice. You can do things exactly the way you want to and make them work for you. It's often easier and way more satisfying to do things in the way that feels most authentic to you.

If you're a business owner, your employees will follow your lead. So when you hire your team, look for people who can take what you have done and make it better than it was before. And if you're working for someone now, show your boss who you are.

Rule #15

GUT CHECK

get into

your intuition

I mposter syndrome is real. And, out of all the bad patterns we can fall into, it is one of the most annoying, and it's incredibly hard to break.

When it comes to all things business, learning to trust my gut has not come easily. And it's not that it comes naturally now, but I know to check in with myself more often. It's become how I look at things: I do a gut check.

It was always much easier for me to trust my gut when it involved something creative, like deciding whether a new fabric or slightly odd color would create design magic or determining which shoe would finish a look at a photo shoot. But if it had to do with money, logistics, production, or technology, I just wanted someone else to make the decisions for me.

I didn't have a formal design education. I didn't go to business school. I never learned to speak corporate and always had to google terms like *low-hanging fruit* and *COB*. There's a reason why movie villains are played by people with severe haircuts wearing serious suits and expensive shiny shoes and who talk about having "skin in the game": they are intimidating as shit.

Whenever I would find myself in a meeting with high-powered magazine editors or high-strung investment bankers, I would have to fight the urge to crawl under the conference room table or—and this would have been worse than hiding under the table—to just smile and nod and listen to them talk and then cut the meeting short without moving any business forward. No matter how confident I was when I walked into the room, once I sat at that table, I started feeling like I had no idea what I was doing. When you don't have the pedigree or the social circle or the jargon, it's easy to feel like you're out of your league. Whatever opinions or advice these people shared, I took as fact. They were the professionals. I was a scrappy bag maker.

LISTEN IN

On the creative side, things were easier—at least at the start. I designed what I wanted and what I thought my friends would want too. Then, as we grew, I became devoted to the message boards and the PurseForum, and I wanted to give the community what they wanted. On top of that, I really respected our account representatives at the showroom and took all of their feedback into consideration, as well as the feedback from the buyers. I wanted to know what our public relations department had to say about things and was always curious if they had spotted any trends bubbling up. And when the team spoke, I listened wholeheartedly. I wanted the collection to be as strong as possible and to make everybody happy.

Welp, you've heard it before, but I'll say it again: you're never going to make everyone happy. I have thousands of sample bags that never saw the light of day to prove it.

How did that happen? The creative stuff—knowing that a bag is good and perfect and right—was supposed to be the easy part for me. But those thousands of samples showed that I was getting it wrong. And I had to hold myself accountable. I accepted that I had gotten to this place, but I wasn't exactly sure how. Eventually, I sat down to examine all of the decisions that had led me here. Were they all mine?

Not exactly.

That same uncomfortable feeling I had experienced in all of those conference rooms? It had sneaked its way into other aspects of my life: I was feeling a tiny version of it, small but still so powerful, all the time. I didn't trust myself anymore.

It got to a point where I couldn't make a single decision. I was way beyond decision fatigue and was into absolute decision avoidance. I felt like I had screwed up too many times. I would find myself faced with a problem, and then I'd turn over the decision-making power to someone else. I didn't trust myself to come up with the answer. I believed that anyone but me would be better, would know what was right.

I wish I could go back into every one of those meetings and remind my baby business self that I was in the room for a reason. I wish I could remind her that the others in the room were the ones who had called her. I wish I could keep her from feeling like she had nothing going for her when she in fact was a successful designer who had built her company starting with a T-shirt. When you find yourself in a situation where you feel in over your head, remind yourself that you are there for a reason and that nobody belongs there more than you.

This state of decision avoidance was miserable. I was miserable. It felt like I was lost, like a pinball ricocheting inside an old arcade machine, smacking up against the rail and then bouncing clear in the other direction. New bag styles weren't selling as we had anticipated they would. People weren't into the clothes, and we couldn't put a finger on why. I had incorporated so much input from so many different perspectives into the collection, and I thought for sure it would have paid off.

I do not regret my big messy failures. I regret that when I knew in my gut something was wrong, even when it was something small, I didn't have enough faith in myself to fight for what I knew was right. I regret the times that I trusted someone else or an outside entity more than I trusted myself. At the end of the day, these choices were in my control.

When you're out of your league, or when you're starting something completely new, of course you will want to look to others for guidance. It's a good move. There will always be someone with more experience than you. Go to these people, seek them out, and listen when they answer your questions and tell you stories from back in the day. If you're bad at finance, don't just trust your gut. Find the expert and get all the details. Ask their opinion. But do so knowing you need to come to decisions on your own. Collect as much information as possible, ask as many experts for their insights as you can, and then synthesize the information so that your decisions are 100 percent your own. Once you have done your research, make the call. Allowing others to help you understand what factors to consider during the decision-making process still allows you to come to your own conclusions.

GIVE YOUR GUT SOME CREDIT

Taking responsibility for my decisions has allowed me to accept and learn from that ownership. There are times when I wish I had made different choices, but for the most part, when I have listened to my gut, I've felt like I was making the best decision based on the information and circumstances of the moment. It's the situations when I have handed the decision-making power over to others or let people tell me what was best for me and my business that have left me wondering if things might have turned out another way.

Negative thinking gets the better of all of us sometimes. The more awareness we have when it comes to recognizing these thoughts as just thoughts and not necessarily as facts or truths, the better we will become at stopping them in their tracks. I ring the alarm when a negative thought creeps in, and I reinforce the opposite. When I'm feeling the effects of imposter syndrome and asking myself, *Who would be better equipped to make this decision?* I immediately change tack and tell myself, *I am the only one who can make this decision. I know my company better than anyone.*

The more attention you give a thought, the stronger it becomes. There are definitely more than a few calligraphic quotes on Instagram and Pinterest reminding us that "Where thought goes, energy flows." (I'm sure you could find that maxim embroidered on a pillow on Etsy without trying very hard.) You're the boss of your mind. Do you want to spend your time thinking that everything is falling apart, or would you rather tell yourself it's going to work out?

Check in with yourself. Go with your gut.

Rule #16

HAVE AN EXPERIMENTAL PHASE

you'll never know

until you try

've been advised against most of the best choices I've made. But my attitude has always been that I might as well try something new.

When I wanted to spend hours on PurseForum cultivating a relationship with the women who were excited about my bags, I was told it was a waste of time. People said that there was no real need for that because the customer wanted to be dictated to by the designer.

So you can imagine the intense amount of eye rolls Uri and I received when I said I wanted to start partnering with bloggers. And there were not only eye rolls, but also true interventions. We had sit-downs with high-powered editors in chief and heads of the biggest department stores around in which they begged us not to associate with such people. "Don't do this," they advised. "You are better than this. You need to be above the bloggers. You need to remain in your ivory tower, untouchable." Yes, those are direct quotes.

Before influencers were called *influencers*, they were called *microbloggers*, and all the cool kids posted photos of their outfits (and breakfasts and cats) on Tumblr. (Merriam-Webster didn't even add the word *influencer* to their dictionary until 2019.) And I knew I wanted to work with these microbloggers directly.

TESTING, TESTING, 1, 2, 3 . . .

Back in the late aughts, social media was like the Wild West. Facebook was only a few years old, and Twitter was just getting started. Before there was Instagram, Tumblr was the platform that combined visuals with short-form text and allowed you to "follow" and "like" different content creators, combining microblogging and social networking into one. People were just getting the hang of it. Very few people (maybe only Ashton Kutcher) knew what the future would hold. But there was a definite possibility that it could become kind of a big deal.

My team and I were always on the lookout for new opportunities and constantly racking our brains to figure out other ways of getting the line in front of people. I know I say it a lot, but really, the feedback I got by spending so much time on Purse-Forum's message boards was crucial when I was just starting out. It showed me how important it was to connect directly with fans of the brand. Our fans in the forums, "Minkettes," as they called themselves, were highly engaged and incredibly direct with their critiques and criticisms. They loved commenting on how obsessed they were with a new style or a certain piece of hardware just as much as they loved ripping a style apart. At least they were honest. Having immediate insight into what was resonating and what wasn't proved to be an incredible tool. The experience trained me to look for other opportunities to get involved with avenues that would keep the lines of communication open and that would keep insights from our girls flowing my way.

If PurseForum taught me how to be in touch with our girls and told me what they were into, blogs gave me pictures of our bags being popular. When blogs first started popping up, we would see photos of our bags out in the streets of Manhattan on the arm of Leandra Medine posing with Chiara Ferragni, or in mirror selfies with Rumi Neely.

In the early days, the old-guard media and retailers made it seem like courting bloggers was letting the trash in. It's crazy to think about that now, since influencers have so much presence and power in the media today. Many magazine editors and most of the fashion elite saw these early bloggers as wannabes or imposters. Most traditional retailers shook their heads. "Does anyone really think we want to see photos of their closets?" they asked. "Who cares what they are wearing?" "Why on earth would they think anyone would want to see them on vacation or enjoying their French toast?" They told me, "We don't know if we can work with you if you're going to work with them."

But I thought I might as well try it.

As a brand, we accepted that we weren't going to have the same path as a standard fashion company, mostly because we kept trying to do that and it would just never work out for us. One way that we kept the brand name out there and built some recognition for ourselves was through getting involved with new technology platforms as early as possible. If we heard about an app or social networking site that seemed like it had any potential at all to do anything, we jumped on it. Sure, that meant that we put resources into endeavors like Vine or Google+ that didn't seem to go anywhere. But it also meant that if things began building momentum, we were already at the party.

Even though it wasn't the popular or cool thing to do, I started getting to know the fashion-blogger scene. I was curious. And I liked what they were doing. I couldn't help it. These were women who were doing their own thing, wearing what they wanted to wear, and making their lives picture-perfect for the camera. I figured the worst-case scenario would be that I gave a few bags away, and the best-case scenario would be that doing so would help me sell some. Seemed like it was worth a shot. Turns out, people did in fact care what these bloggers had to say.

In the summer of 2010, we needed to figure out a way to let everyone know that our fall collection was launching on the website. We invited the bloggers that we had friendly relationships with for a weekend in the Hamptons. They would be kept super comfy for a summer getaway with a cook, stocked kitchen, and housekeeper, and in exchange they would test-drive all the new clothing and accessories, style it their way, and snap tons of pics for their blogs and our feed and website. Over the course of that weekend, I felt like I got a sneak peak of the future. I was used to chatting with editors and stylists about what they were working on and what trends they were seeing bubble up. There was none of that. There were only cool girls who woke up and got selfie-ready, then proceeded to document their lives from their morning matcha latte till their sunset glass of rosé. It was definitely different. I really began to embrace the idea of the fashion blogger—especially this crew. Everyone was just starting out, and their followings were small compared to what they are today, but they had style, they had their own unique points of view, and most refreshing of all was that they had fun. First like!

I know it sounds cliché, but it's true what they say about risks: take them. If you are trying to create something new, and you're doing the same thing over and over again in the same way and banging your head against the wall because it's not working, there's your answer. Doing the same thing repeatedly while expecting to get a different result each time creates deep frustration and unrest. It will drive you crazy. If you're aiming to bring something fresh, new, and different into the world, go for it. Do it differently. Try it your way. If you have nothing to lose, then why not? You already know that nothing is going to happen if you don't do it, so you might as well try.

There's a touch of the give-it-a-whirl approach in most things my team and I do. As often as circumstances have forced us to be innovative in the past, we really like being intentionally innovative too. But when the options are to either attempt to stay the course and do what everyone else is doing or to open up to the possibilities of things being better, different, and special, I'll take door number two every time.

OPEN DOORS

When it came time to open a store in New York, we needed a big give-it-a-whirl mindset. If I ever thought anything would give me that I-have-arrived feeling, it would be having my own flagship boutique in SoHo. In 2014, opening one was the next logical step, which felt really exciting, but at the same time, it was going to be an enormous undertaking and a huge financial risk. In a word: eek. In two words: holy shit.

There were generally two directions everyone told us we had to go. The first direction was super-high-end luxury. It would have been fun and glamorous to try this out, but it didn't really seem like us. We were more for the person who knew about the ultimate bag, dress, or shoe of the season but who wasn't going to spend all of her rent money on a purchase. Plus, if there was any chance that I was going to feel out of my league walking into my own store, then I would have to assume a lot of other women would feel that way too. The other direction we were told we could go was the more-is-more approach. This is the feeling you get when you walk into a fast-fashion shop and you're wowed by the sheer volume of stuff that is in front of your face. There's easy access and no shortage of options; all of it could be yours. That sort of thing. The problem with that option was that nothing would ever feel special.

We were going to have to come up with a third direction. What could we possibly create that would make the store worth all of the time, work, and money that it was going to require?

I wasn't sure exactly what our flagship boutique would be, but I was very clear on what it would not be. There was absolutely no way that it could be a regular old boring store. I didn't want to waste everyone's time—not the shoppers', not my team's, and not my own. If it was going to be just another shop where a perky salesperson greeted you with a plastic water bottle that was either a little too warm or a little too cold before you wandered from clothing rack to clothing rack hoping to find something while the salesperson pretended not to stare at you from an uncomfortable distance, there would be no point.

Uri and I started out by deciding what we didn't want in order to get to what we wanted. As a devoted shopper myself, I wanted a better sales experience. When I walked into a store, I wanted to know all of my options. I wanted to see what the designer had been thinking. In other stores, when I needed another size of something I thought I might like, I found that it was always hard to get a salesperson's attention, and it was always very awkward to have a conversation through a dressing room door while half-naked. I knew I couldn't possibly be the only person who felt these things.

After airing all our grievances with how blah and formulaic shopping had become, we turned to technology. Uri has always been tuned into the tech space, so he had tons of futuristic-sounding solutions to my real-world problems. What if the walls were screens? What if we had an app that could alert the sales team to the shoppers' actual needs? What if people entered a code and we sent the shoes out on a conveyor belt? Some of our ideas ventured into sci-fi territory, but all of it pushed the brand and the retail experience into the future in just the right ways.

When we finally opened our doors, we weren't just opening a Rebecca Minkoff store; we were opening The. Store. Of. The. Future. Ba-ba-baaaaa! We set it up so that when you entered and checked in on our mobile app, your personal profile would be sent to the store associates so they could understand you better and actually be helpful. Instead of art, we did a connected wall that displayed content from our shows, shoots, and social media channels. Shoppers could tap the wall to browse the collection, request a fitting room, or order a drink. It was very *The Jetsons*. The fitting-room mirrors were connected screens as well, and they used radio-frequency identification to track the tags on what the shopper had brought in, which allowed the system to guess other sizes she might need and make product recommendations based on past purchases. And if the shopper wanted anything, all she had to do was touch the screen.

It wasn't the same old, same old. And that's what everyone seemed to love about it—especially me.

If you look around, you will see the steps that people have taken to get where they are. And if you study their moves closely enough, you can figure out what you need to do too. But if you're just following others and doing the same things, you're likely going to get the same results, the same successes, and the same failures along the way.

It's taken me years to realize that I could do things in exactly the way that felt best for the brand and ultimately for me. As an entrepreneur, you enter into a field that has a certain set of rules or a way of doing things that were established by the people who succeeded by doing things those ways. But did those people just follow the rules, or were they the pioneers? What was happening before they came onto the scene? Each person who helped pave the way was an innovator. Why can't you be one too?

Rule #17

GET FRIENDLY WITH FAILURE

sometimes you win;

sometimes you learn

So I have some bad news for you: If you haven't noticed, things are going to go wrong. So very, very wrong. It's good to get used to this idea now. That way you're not shocked when it happens the first time, or the tenth. Know it's coming. There will be highs, and there will be lows. The hits are going to come, if not today, then tomorrow, or the day after that. If messing up has taught me anything, it's that when you fail (not *if*, but *when*), you have to face failure head-on.

THE ART OF NOT FREAKING OUT

When the business was really starting to pick up momentum, I was sitting in Paris at the most glamorous restaurant I had ever been to in my life. The president of my company and I had spent the day in back-to-back-to-back sales meetings, showing the new collection to buyers from across Europe, and it felt incredible to sit down. The insanely decadent truffle pasta and ridiculously delicious champagne made the nonstop workday all worth it. We were surrounded by impeccably dressed fashion people chattering in French, and I was sure they were talking about really big, really chic, important fashion things. With the time change, New York was still working while we were at dinner, so I checked my emails from time to time, as one does. And then an email from my brother came through with no subject, but the preview text read, "The bank says they are done." It was like time and space came screeching to a halt. The news wasn't entirely unexpected, but to actually face the moment when the bank was no longer going to advance us funds for production and everything else was terrifying.

The company had reached a point in our feverish growth escalation where the amount of money that we had coming in as an advance from the bank to fund future orders was more than the amount of money we had coming in for existing orders. The bank wasn't willing to keep that up. But without that advance, we couldn't pay for our next round of deliveries, and if we didn't cover that, then the deliveries wouldn't ship, and we wouldn't have anything for people to order. It was a serious avalanche.

I had to fight the urge to freak out.

The reality of this perfect moment was that there were an unlimited number of worse scenarios that I could have been going through. It might sound fatalistic, but I like to imagine what rock bottom looks like so that I can come back to reality. Like, what if I were a well-known designer and no one wanted to work with me ever again because I went bankrupt? Or what if we couldn't convince the banks to float us just a little while longer, and our cash flow ran dry and we had to lay off our entire team? It could mean having to hang up our bags and call it a day. Maybe the company I poured my blood, sweat, and tears into was going to end up in the hands of a coldhearted liquidator. Maybe it was over for me in fashion and I was going to head back to Florida and start answering the phones at my dad's office. I knew at least he would hire me.

To get to this point of being able to face failure without completely losing my shit, I had to fail a lot. Like, a lot a lot. There was that one time my phone rang and it was a buyer from one of the coolest boutiques in Los Angeles calling to tell me that the only thing wrong with their first order was absolutely everything. The pieces weren't labeled correctly, nothing had been packed according to their guidelines, and every piece reeked of cigarette smoke. (Remember my go-to Garment District production guy? Well, he smoked at least two packs a day. And the proof was in the boxes that were currently making one of the coolest shops in Los Angeles smell like an ashtray.) I wanted to barf, mostly from the embarrassment of it all. They were canceling their check and shipping everything back. That was fun. And then there was the phase where a junior social media assistant told me that no one wanted to see my real life because it was boring and so were pictures of my kids. I believe her exact words were, "Our customer is twenty-seven. Don't show her your real life!" Against my gut, we listened. Our engagement plummeted. It turned out that our girl wanted to see this side of the brand, not some perfectly curated images of a model that's unattainable. I ended up scrapping that idea and going back to sharing what was authentic to the brand and me.

The truth of the matter was, whatever happened, I was going to be okay. Even if I was devastated, I was going to make it through to the other side. I found my center. I reminded myself that they could take my company, they could take my apartment, but they couldn't take my husband or my kids. At that moment, I knew that what mattered most were those that I loved and cherished—they were the only things that were irreplaceable.

And in that instant, I knew that no matter what happened, I would bounce back. I was going to be okay. I would figure it out. Whatever happened, no one could take away the things that were the most precious to me.

Knowing the stakes and what I had the potential to lose was all the motivation I needed to get down to business. I could have thrown some Euros on the table and run out of the restaurant like my hair was on fire, but having gone through my worst-case scenarios in my head, I knew that there was nothing I could do to change the situation at that very moment, so I decided to finish my extremely delicious plate of pasta. I ordered two more glasses of champagne. (Priorities, right?) When I was finished, I went back to my hotel room and called my brother. It wasn't time to fall apart. It was time to get to work.

If you looked at just a snapshot of the numbers on paper, without taking anything else into account, business did not look great. We were a big brand with lots of overhead and tons of expansion. Sometimes there are just moments in your business life where you have way more money going out than you do coming in. The highs and lows are all part of the ride. There was no PowerPoint in the world that would convince a hard-line businessperson that flowing us more cash would be a brilliant idea.

WE'RE ONLY HUMAN

When you're in a jam like that, you need people to act from their human goodness. My brother and I had spent years building our personal relationships so that when things didn't look great on paper, we'd be able to open the lines of communication to paint a bigger, more complete picture of the reality of what was really happening. Michael (our banking partner) and I had been working together for close to a decade. He had made the decision to support the business when we were just starting out, and he certainly bought into the potential and the dream.

I was so grateful for him taking a chance on me that I made a concerted effort to make sure he was included in everything— not just the annual report emails. There was (and still is) a seat for him in the front row at every show, and there were always invites to all the parties and events we threw. When he was fundraising for charities that were important to him, we made donations or even hosted. He came along for every part of the journey. When we faced hardship or achieved a tough accomplishment as a brand, he was emotionally invested too. I knew I needed to make the call.

On the phone with Michael and Uri, the discussion was much more than just "here's the problem; please solve it with more cash." Over the course of a few hours, we went over our entire strategy, including where we had come from, where we saw the brand going, and how we had gotten ourselves into this mess in the first place.

Once Michael was able to get a better handle on the situation from a bird's-eye view, we were able to envision our very bright, very sunny possible future, though we knew we would only be able to get there with his help. Before long, the three of us started getting somewhere closer to a solution. And eventually, with a lot of tough questions and honest answers, we came to a decision. It wasn't money or numbers that saved us in the end. It was our long-standing relationship and authentic connection. No person or brand can win alone. There are a lot of people who have made my dream come true, and we all wanted, and continue to want, the brand to win.

Being able to face a failure this big and not completely fall apart does not come easily. I had to fail a lot to get this good at it. You have to go through the exercise of confronting it. Each time you have a setback or a situation that seems uncomfortable, stare it in the face. Go on and look it in the eye. Snuggle up to it. Don't be afraid to explore it, touch it, and feel it—really get in there.

Don't panic; evaluate the situation. Don't judge it. Look at it objectively. What are the mechanics? What's really going on? How exactly did you get here? What's the very worst that can happen? What is your biggest fear? What would that be like? Is that the end of the world? Is it really so bad after all? Settle into the feeling of being unsettled, that woozy moment of truly not knowing what to expect or what exactly is going to come next. The only way you're going to get out of it is if you really understand where you are and what you're dealing with. Then you can start asking questions, like, What's missing from this picture? and What needs to change?

By failing over and over again, I've been able to practice being more analytical when I am dealing with problems and less personal, less emotional, and less reactive. You're going to fail as much as you succeed in business, and that's part of the journey. Bad things happening is not the exception; it's the norm. When you don't take failure personally, it's easier to come up with solutions. It's just business. You've got to have resilience.

So when things blow up in your face, instead of being shocked or falling apart, you can think, *Oh yeah, Rebecca told me things like this would happen. What's next?* It might feel like the sky is falling, and it might be, but what are you going to do? Stand there and freak out while you get lost in the clouds, or look up and see what's left? What matters most is what comes next, how you handle it, and what you learn from it.

No matter how many times you fall, you have to get back up again with a smile on your face.

Rule #18

COLLAB OVER COMPETE

there's always

enough success

to go around

Behind every successful woman is a tribe of women who have her back. But meeting these women can be tougher than it should be.

When building the business, I spent a lot of time on my own. If you think the media makes the fashion world seem competitive, then you're getting the right impression. *The Devil Wears Prada* was basically a documentary. There were many days that I spent solo, schlepping fabric bolts and zippers around the Garment District, and there were many nights I spent sitting alone clipping chain straps to MAB clutches.

Around 2016, I was talking to a friend about how I felt a lack of connection and community in fashion. I wanted to get past the cliquish, bold-faced name scene and find some like-minded professional women who were up for exchanging ideas and sharing experiences. If we were all in this together, why were we all going through so much alone? The solution to feeling disconnected was simple: we needed to connect.

CALLING ALL SUPERWOMEN

I decided to host a dinner at our flagship store in SoHo. I was going to cast a wide net into the sea of women I respected in the industry and see who showed up. Everyone on my list was a woman that I admired, so I called it the Superwomen dinner. Some were friends, some were work acquaintances, some were work crushes. They worked in a range of industries, but they were all incredibly passionate and devoted to whatever it was they spent their time on.

My biggest fear was that no one would show up. My second biggest fear was that everyone would leave before dessert. But all eighteen women who were invited and RSVP'd yes did indeed come. And everyone stayed until the last drop of wine had been drunk. To get the conversation going, I asked every guest to share one thing: something surprising about herself. It got the group talking about the good stuff fast, rather than having too many pleasantries and small talk eat up precious minutes of our time together. (Why talk about the weather when you can go deep? That's what people will remember.)

After that first dinner, I knew I was onto something. I felt energized by this group of women. The evening began with a sense of curiosity. This was a group that didn't always run in the same circle. Curiosity quickly became interest, which ultimately became the support that each of us needed.

It felt so good to have a place where women could share what was going on in their professional worlds with other women who could relate. We planned another dinner, then another, and another after that. Once the Superwomen ball got rolling, we did fireside chats, cohosted dinners at Soho House, and started a dedicated Instagram account to keep everyone connected.

This was where I learned to be vulnerable. It was where I learned to see what I could do to help support other women and how the power of our network could become a source of success for all of us. I wanted every woman at the table to be able to take away the feeling that she was not alone, that we were all struggling, too, and that we could be there for each other and lift each other up.

As much as I loved it—which was a lot—I couldn't help but think there was something a little bit off about it. It was amazing to sit around a table with some of the women who were shaping media, culture, fashion, music, art, and social change, but invite-only events are exclusive by default. The only people who were benefiting from the exchanging of ideas, the knowledge, the empathy, and the laughs were the people who were there. Sharing snippets on social media just wasn't enough.

I started thinking a lot about how to better unite us and how to unite more of us—how to involve anyone who wanted to participate. I wanted to connect the entrepreneurs I was inspired by, the thought leaders and creatives changing our culture for the better, and all the open-minded, wholehearted people out there who were doing their best to make the most out of every day. I wanted to find a space to further the goals I had for myself and for all women. I wanted to encourage a strong sense of fearlessness, to help us ready ourselves for those moments when we needed it most.

Let's get one thing straight: Being fearless doesn't mean you don't have fear. It means that as you look fear head-on, shaking in your boots, you do what's scaring you anyway. Maybe that's asking for a deserved raise, breaking up with a significant other, resigning from a job to pursue something new, or starting your own company. Whatever it is, in a world where men find encouragement in every corner, women need the same encouragement, and we need to know that there are other women out there who are dealing with the same sorts of issues. It's a crazy ride, and the best way to experience it is through our stories, differences, and individualities—from one superwoman to another.

That's where the *Superwomen* podcast came in. Once it launched, everyone could listen in on the conversations that were happening behind closed doors and could get the benefits of being in the room with not only some of the biggest change makers around but also women from all walks who lead their lives with fearlessness and resilience. Getting to interview these incredibly accomplished and fascinating women never, ever gets old.

THINK BIG, THEN BIGGER

Through the Superwomen gatherings, I met a few women who were involved with the New York State Council on Women and Girls, an organization that connects the government and the private sector with a mission to lift women up and fight for the rights that everyone should be afforded. The women involved had academic, business, media, nonprofit, and advocacy backgrounds, and they joined together to take action and make a real impact. It was right up my alley. Being invited to participate was one of the greatest honors of my life.

In addition to handling the brain trust side of things, the council members were invited to bring up any initiatives they felt would be aligned with the organization's greater mission. One such idea had been kicking around in my head for a while.

When I became a mom, I started paying much more attention to the labels on food and beauty products, scanning for the nasty chemicals that I wanted to avoid and the business ethics I wanted to support. The cute little rabbit icon told me a product was cruelty-free, and a sprout icon let me know if something was non-GMO or responsibly farmed. There was a made-in-New-York symbol that people really liked. Why couldn't we have one for women-owned businesses? It could be stamped onto products of any kind, and it would allow people to see where their money was going and to support women through their own companies. People want to make educated decisions, and this would help them do so. I proposed the idea and everyone seemed into it, but it ended the way that many things do in government: tangled in lots of red tape.

GO TIME

When I got back from maternity leave in April 2018, I realized very quickly that I was not as needed. I had never had a real don't-check-your-email maternity leave and thought that, for my last baby, the priority was going to be me. To be honest, I was also tired. I was mentally spent. It had been a long and hard pregnancy and I was not at the top of my game. The good news was that I had staffed up properly before taking my break. The bad news was, everything was running like a well-oiled machine without me.

Since I wasn't spending all my time with design worrying about the fabric content of a T-shirt or the Pantone color blue that would be "just right," I started filling my calendar with speaking engagements and events. I loved connecting with people, so I always said yes (and still do) whenever I was asked to speak, but then I would find myself under the lights on a propped-up stage, telling the same story I had told at a million other events. This wasn't because I didn't have other stories to tell, but because that was the entry point for at least part of the crowd. I would go home wondering if I had helped anyone at all or if they were just as lost when they left as they had been when they came in, with the only difference being that they now possessed a gift bag. The more panels I did, the more bored I got. By May, I wanted—and needed—to do something bigger with my time.

I was over the idea of "business as usual." When the Women and Girls council would get together, we would talk endlessly about the wage gap and other inequalities that women faced in the workforce. What I knew to be true was that, from purchasing decisions to employment opportunities, women are an incredible and undeniable force. When we enable and empower female-owned and female-led companies, we're positively impacting our communities, both socially and economically. Women reinvest income in their families and communities at a higher rate than men. It's just the way it is. So I knew that if we were able to increase the wealth and opportunities for women-owned businesses, we would be changing the world for the better in a true and meaningful way—a way that could have a generational impact. I wanted to go beyond the basics of hiring women, buying from female-owned brands, and spreading the word. I wanted to bring in the real-life connection that I felt was missing when I was just starting out and that I felt was still missing.

I revived my idea to establish a woman-made seal and brought it back to the council to pick up where we had left off. It was more important to me than ever. And I had the bandwidth to take it on. Thanks to all the government stuff, my efforts went nowhere fast. Then a very smart lady told me I should just go on and do it myself.

In September 2018, I launched the Female Founder Collective, a network of women supporting women. It's a platform for women to connect with other women in order to share re-sources and have conversations that help grow and support their companies and careers.

The response was unlike anything I had seen before. It turned out that I wasn't the only one who was searching for like minds. As of this writing, we have over nine thousand members and our seal is on over three million products. With this group, we are able to offer an alternative to the days when people kept their Rolodexes locked away and when secrets to success were truly secret and not just clickbait headlines. We all want what's best for each other, and the strength of that is real.

THE REACH BACK

So often, we get wrapped up in a competition that isn't even happening. For so long, there were few (if any) seats at the table for women, and it created a scarcity mindset that lingers today. I value the path that was paved by the women who came before me who fought and continue to fight for equality. It's when women come together that change is catalyzed.

Falling into a comparison trap is like getting your heel stuck in the sidewalk grate in New York City: you have to deal with it and move on. Instead of seeing someone's success and feeling jealous or defeated, look at it as proof of concept and cheer her on. She's proving that it's possible, which means it's possible for you too. It is crucial that we look to each other for support since mainstream media has been leaving women out of the story for so long.

When women succeed, we all look good. So when you make it to the top, look down and reach back for the women coming up behind you.

Whether you have a wide net of contacts or just a few people that you feel like you can easily relate to and whose opinion you trust and respect, send out a group email and see who is down to start a group. You can meet weekly, monthly, seasonally— whatever works for you. When women work together, anything is possible.

Rule #19

GO BEYOND BURNOUT

work can be

self-care too

When it comes to work, burnout is a really hot topic. (How could it not be?) The goal is to be doing something that you love, a job that you're completely passionate about that helps you put your vision into the world or that aligns with your purpose, or, even better, both. So if we are all chasing our dreams, why are we all so burned out all the time? Doing your thing should lift you up, not bring you down.

It seems like the common understanding now is that we are all going to deal with burnout. And then we have to figure out how to do enough self-care to get ourselves back together so that we can jump right back into whatever was burning us out. To me, that seems like a cycle. Do the same thing, get burned out in the same way, apply a face mask in a salt bath while drinking a turmeric latte, repeat.

Instead of only asking ourselves what it is going to take to feel better after getting to a breaking point, what if we dealt with what's burning us out in the first place? Burnout comes from living in a constant state of stress. There is no scented candle in the world that will make that feeling go away.

GIVE IT A NAME

Just as each pregnancy, each birth, and each child is so completely different, so is returning to work after maternity leave. You never know what you're going to get.

When I went back to work with Luca, I was excited. I was high on motherhood and felt like I could conquer the world. I didn't really miss a beat, even answering emails from my hospital bed like it was no biggie. I wound up cutting it short and took six weeks away from the office instead of the full three months. I felt like we were so new, and still a very lean team so I had to go back, but I didn't mind.

While I was pregnant with Bowie, we decided to put a few key people in place so that I didn't feel the pressure to rush back and could get acclimated to life with two kids. The idea of staffing up worked in theory. After she was born, while I wasn't completely offline, snuggled up in babyland, I didn't have to be attached to my phone 24/7 as I had been the first time around. When I did hear news from the office or follow an email thread to its end, I started to get the sense that there was something up. I couldn't quite put my finger on it at first, but slowly I realized that with a few key decisions, the company was starting to change course. In my absence, those hires started taking things in a very different direction without me.

When my maternity leave was up and the day came for me to go back in, I could barely get out of bed. Work was the last place that I wanted to be. It felt horrible to dread going into the office where my name was on the door, especially when it used to fill me up so much that I would work around the clock whenever I was. I would try to voice my concerns, and in response everyone would chalk it up to just being really burned out. After all the years I had put in, with two kids at home now, with so much on my plate for so long . . . the people around me seemed to be able to come up with countless reasons for my so-called burnout.

But how do you get burned out from a job when you haven't worked for three months? I knew I had to go deeper and figure out what was really going on.

Underneath what everyone wanted to label *burnout*, for which they wanted to pass some aromatherapy my way, was something much more complicated, something a massage could never solve. When you love to express yourself creatively but you're spending your days pushing papers around, your heart is going to start to feel it. And that's where I was: disappointed, disillusioned, and disheartened. This is when I found out I had a real "black widow" situation on my hands. A team member we had hired really didn't see the need for me to be around. This dynamic made work miserable. I had the energy to devote to design, marketing, and really any aspect of the business where I could get involved, but the negative vibes were shutting down any momentum that I could muster. Once it became clear to me that someone was intentionally making life more difficult than it needed to be, I knew that eventually others at the company would see what was really going on too. It might take a while, but eventually the truth always comes out. I made up my mind that instead of accepting this pseudo diagnosis of burnout and checking out, I would double down. And it worked.

With Nico, things were different but I was more prepared and had a new perspective on returning to work. This time, it wasn't that I didn't want to go back, it was that I didn't completely recognize what the company had grown into. It was big, which was amazing. But where did I fit in? The company needed full-time focus and attention in so many different departments that I knew deep down I could not do it all on my own anymore. There were many people whose job it was to do all the things that I had done when I was just starting out on my own. If I wanted to have any semblance of a personal life, I had to let the leaders we hired do their jobs. What I had worked so hard to build was now a place where I would have to reevaluate and rework where I could be the biggest asset. And maybe it meant I didn't get to spend all day in the design room anymore work-ing with the team on every detail; maybe it meant I needed to be more forward-facing and getting back to my girls—the cus-tomers. I knew deep down that the future of our company and its growth had to come from this move, and so as hard as it was, I pulled on my big-girl pants after a month or so of being bummed out and dove in.

Once I put my finger on where I really was, then I could fig-ure out how to get myself to where I wanted to be—not just for an afternoon, but for good. After taking a good look at what was happening at work, I was able to make a plan for how I was going to work my way back in. It wasn't all pretty. I needed to decide who should stay, who should go (this was a big one), what my responsibilities were, what others needed to take care of, and really redefine my daily role. It was on me if I wanted it to be. Just having the plan to make a plan lifted the fog. Think-ing about what needed to shift and how I was going to make it happen completely energized me. I had a purpose, I'd recon-nected with my passion, and I was ready to go. I didn't need to take a break; I needed to dive back in.

Reigniting my passion was all the self-care I needed.

WHAT WORKS FOR ME

People talk more about how to treat burnout than what causes it or even how to avoid it. I'm constantly asked about my self-care routine. At almost every panel now, someone wants to know how I make time for myself or recharge.

My version of self-care is getting nine hours of sleep. But I get seven. It's taking my vitamins and then drinking a giant coffee. It's getting as much fresh air and exercise as I can, which is sometimes none. To get ready, I wash my face and slather on creams just like everybody else who is trying not to look like a zombie — not easy when you have three kids. I will spritz on my fragrance because it reminds me of why I do so much of what I do. One false eyelash cluster at the end of each of my lash lines makes a huge difference, and so does Botox. Every night, I take my supplements and pound a glass of Calm, a magnesium-based anti-stress drink (it complements my earlier anti-stress drinks, like, for instance, a margarita). The last thing I do before I close my eyes is check my phone and then put it on airplane mode. Sometimes after I kiss Gavin.

I realize some people might think this is really bad. We've all heard about the importance of keeping your phone outside the bedroom, but I'd rather not have to walk all the way to the kitchen to check my email when I wake up. Shutting down is not for everyone, and that's okay. These small actions don't feel like indulgences; they're basic maintenance (except maybe the Botox). I am a serial entrepreneur and am married with three kids. I haven't had "me-time" since 2011, when Luca was born, and I've just accepted it.

But no matter what, I show up for work. I get everything that is mission-critical done. I can't go to bed with to-dos hanging over my head. I live to zero out my inbox. (JK, it's hovering at under three hundred right now and only because I decided to close my eyes and delete anything a year or more old.) That's what makes me feel good. Doing what needs to be done is the best stress reliever there is.

REEVALUATE

Now, if you're really feeling burned out, what's behind your burnout? You have to look at where your energy is going. Do you really love your job? If yes, great. But what is it about it that's sucking you dry rather than filling you up? Is it a new project? Is it an issue with a colleague? Bad work environments lead to burnout just as easily as a bad project or having too much on your plate. External life factors, unrelated to work, can make the work itself feel less inspiring. Perhaps you're taking care of an ill family member and no one at work seems to be supportive. That could make you feel burned out too. Whenever possible, surround yourself with people who get it.

And if you don't love your job anymore, can you make a change? Switching careers or getting a new gig isn't always an easy or realistic option, but you do have the power to change your perspective. There's that oldie but goodie: work to live or live to work. If you're burned out, try flipping from live to work to work to live for a few months: you'd be surprised at how many people actually find it easier to be at work once they stop worrying about every little detail and stop overthinking every interaction. When they just focus on getting the job done and then go home, they are often just as productive (if not more), and their lives outside of work are infinitely more enjoyable. Forcing yourself to take the pressure off of work, off of being amazing every day, for just a few months can help you feel a little less crisp around the edges.

Your life should give you life. It shouldn't exhaust you. Most of your days should not be draining. You should not feel like you are running on empty just by living this life you set out to live. Self-care is not the answer. Self-reflection is. Self-care is just what you need, when you need it, to help you heal in small ways and move forward toward the next day. Self-care without self-reflection, however, is more of a Band-Aid than a cure-all — you still need to get to the bottom of what's causing the burn-out. A beauty mask and a glass of wine can be great. But a beauty mask and a glass of wine and enough time to sit there to tap into why you are feeling rough? That's true self-care.

Rule #20

FORGET ABOUT BALANCE

optimize your

life for you

D id you hear the one about the working mom with three kids? No, you didn't. She's the last person on earth who has time to mess around with a bad joke like this.

When it comes to women and work, one of the biggest buzzwords of our time is *balance*. (Why don't guys get asked how they're balancing everything?) Whoever got that term to start trending never tried to divide the twenty-four-hour day between a family that needs you eighteen hours a day and a job that requires teams in twelve time zones.

I gave up on ever trying to achieve balance a long time ago. We all have a variety of roles and passions, and it's that combination that makes our lives rich. It's also what makes balance unattainable, and it's why I strive for life design instead. As an entrepreneur and a mother and a woman with a life outside of those two things as well, balance just seemed like a losing proposition from the get-go. Balance comes down to how you prioritize your personal and professional lives and how much one crosses over into the other. For me, they are both equally important and they cross over constantly. My family is life. My work is life. Instead of trying to balance the two, I've just come to terms with the fact that I need to be flexible.

PRESENCE IS THE PRESENT

One summer we took a family vacation a month before Fashion Week. The timing couldn't have been worse, but it was the only window in the calendar where Gavin's schedule, the kids' school schedule, and my schedule sort of lined up. We hadn't taken a trip together in ages, and I thought the change of scenery would energize us before we all had to return to our regular day-to-day.

Cut to me working the entire trip. One night, while I was putting Bowie to bed, she said, "Mommy, you're not really acting like my mommy right now." I felt like I had been punched in the gut. She was right. I had been attached to my phone or hiding behind my laptop for days. I apologized to her and told her that in two more days, I would be back to being her mommy again. It was awful.

When you're trying to do it all, days when you feel pulled in a million different directions are inevitable and unavoidable, and ultimately they are reminders to make sure that your priorities—whatever they may be for you—are in check. The day before the Female Founder Collective's biggest event of the year, my son Luca woke up with half his face swollen. I couldn't take any more time off. My other son, Nico, had just had major surgery five days earlier, and I still hadn't had a moment to catch up with everything that I'd had to hit pause on while I was fully focused on him. I was panicking not only as a parent, but also as the founder of a nonprofit that needed me to be present for this event, with over three hundred guests confirmed to attend.

When it was determined that Luca would need a major dental procedure, I was torn. The timing was terrible—Gavin was at work shooting a commercial several states away and I hated the idea of my son being in pain and neither of us being there with him. This is where I had to choose between my son and a cause I believe in. Thankfully, someone close to our family stepped in to help out, and I knew Luca was in good hands.

As a leader, you can't expect your team to take on what you know is your responsibility, and as a parent your job is to be there for your children at all times. In that moment, these two realities clashed for me, and *balance* was the last word I wanted to think about. The awful feeling of not being with Luca stayed with me all day, but I was constantly on the phone consoling him. In between coordinating with the dentist and keeping it together at work to do everything we needed to do to prep for our peak event, I kept reminding myself that he was in good hands, and I knew it was true.

For us working parents, it's common to want to do it all. We want to make the cute bento box lunches with the sliced apples that look like rabbits and a rainbow of chopped veggies. We want to take the meeting and do the deal and nail the interview. But sometimes we dial into a video conference with baby food on our sweatpants, and that's just the reality of it all. The only way I could find my way through being pulled in so many different directions was to accept my feelings about my work life and family life and to know that sometimes I was going to feel rotten and that things would feel like they just sucked. I just had to get comfortable with the fact that I was going to spend a fair amount of time feeling guilty—guilty that I wasn't with my kids when I was at work, guilty I put last night's pizza in their lunch boxes, guilty I had to reschedule a call because I needed to get my baby to nap. There is no winning; there is only going with the flow. If you start to feel those guilty feelings creeping in, remember that you don't have to be perfect, you just have to do your best.

Part of striving for flexibility is getting comfortable with finding some support and solutions. Motherhood continues to be the most transformative experience of my life. I'm grateful to my children and all the extraordinary mothers out there who inspire me for making the journey so special. But sometimes you just have to call for backup, whether it's from your partner, a family member, a babysitter, or Elmo via the good old-fashioned TV. Knowing where to look and asking for what you need when you need it helps take the pressure off. The more you do it, the more you'll see that it's okay. You can be a serious professional and a loving mom without doing every single thing in both arenas all by yourself.

One of the biggest barriers to being present—whether you are dealing with work or spending time with your family at home—is worrying about what's going on wherever you are not. It takes you out of the moment. I've learned that I can't be a present parent if I work 120-hour weeks and that I can't accomplish what I want to professionally if I'm watching the baby monitor all day. Motherhood led me to push back on the societal expectations and demands on our time in ways I never did before having kids. I started leaving the office at 6:00 p.m., skipping out on evening events, and keeping work at bay on the weekends so that I could be more in the mom zone. But this was okay, because having more structure around my time away from the office made me want to maximize my time when I was there.

There is always a lot on the line. In an unpredictable world, you're never going to be able to achieve balance. Life has too many surprises; there's no way to know where your energy is going to be needed day after day. When your attention needs to shift, so does your approach. That's why life design works. What do you want your life to look like? What is most important to you? What do you need? What are your deal-breakers? Reevaluate as you go. You know change is coming, so be adaptable. Work may demand your full attention. Your friends might need you in the middle of the night. And the needs of your family can be completely different from one day to the next. Accept this, and be ready for whatever life throws your way.

To me, the big picture is most important. When I see the smile on my son's face after he takes a bow at his pre-K concert, it makes missing that meeting worth it. And when I feel bad for missing dinner, I remind myself that, one day, my daughter will see everything I have been able to accomplish, and she will know that anything is possible.

There is no such thing as achieving perfect equilibrium. Life can feel manageable, healthy, and totally under control when you're spending time on the things that matter to you. A balancing act is just that—an act.

Rule #21

IT'S ENDLESS

success is being

able to keep going

After decades of doing what I love, I'm still running after success. The goalposts are always moving. Sometimes we think, *If I just get here, I'll feel like I've made it.* But it doesn't work that way.

When COVID-19 swept the globe, it decimated our company. Roughly half of our business was gone. Virtually all of our wholesale orders were canceled, and there was no chance of any new orders coming in. Things were unraveling fast; if we were going to recover at all, whatever was going to happen needed to happen even faster.

In order to survive, we needed to change almost everything about how we were operating. For the first time in our history as a company, we didn't have a wholesale business. As terrifying as that was, we realized that it meant we were free to focus our complete and undivided attention on our own e-commerce business. Our next step was to rightsize our inventory, committing to manufacture only the goods that we felt really represented our brand. Then we had to completely rethink what marketing and influence looked like. Without being able to partner with social media influencers and talent on creative collateral like photos and videos, I was going to put myself out there again as the designer and woman behind the brand. It was up to me to reignite a closer and deeper relationship with our customer, figuring out how to delight her, entertain her, take her mind off of things, and be there for her as we all experienced this unprecedented new reality. We became vulnerable as a brand, letting people into the truth of my everyday life. I was not in a penthouse making pumpkin bread. I was hunkered down with my family working sixteen hours a day, juggling distance learning and diaper changes with Gavin, living for my morning coffee and evening (afternoon?) wine, and trying to figure out TikTok just like everybody else.

It's true that our business will never be the same, but we're on track now, and we're building something even better, stronger, and more authentic to the brand I want to be. The proof for us was immediate: stronger website sales, higher engagement, more communication with our customers and community, a clear, defined aesthetic in our design choices and collection overall. Our approach and track might be different now, but that's evolution.

We are here in large part because we used the rules I have shared in this book to navigate these unprecedented times and ride the waves of unpredictability. Talk about fear. With so much on the line for me, my family, my business, and the world, every day was a new opportunity to put these rules into action. We have rewritten what it means to be a business, how to collaborate and unite, and what it takes to make it in a pandemic economy—and even to thrive.

I hope that you have found something in these pages to take with you as you creatively and courageously make your way in the world. And that you're able to reach your loftiest goals while you're at it.

Before you go, I have just one more rule for you: remember that this path is endless. Which means the possibilities are endless too. Feel your fears. Learn to understand what they are trying to show you. And push them aside when they are holding you back. There is always something more to do, to learn, and to see.

Be thankful for what you have. Be fearless for what you want.

love,
Rebecca

Rule #22

BONUS CHAPTER

Ah, 2025—four years have flown by since I first put pen to paper and unleashed *Fearless* upon the world. And let me tell you, it's been a whirlwind ride. Meeting the incredible women whose lives have been touched by my words has been both humbling and downright exciting. It's like a validation of all those late-night writing sessions and moments of self-doubt–knowing that something I observed, experienced, and shared has resonated so deeply with others is nothing short of magical.

But let's talk about what's really shaken things up since then. Picture this: December 2021 rolls around, and just when we thought we were catching our breath post-COVID, bam! We're hit with a curveball straight out of left field—supply chain issues from hell. I'm talking the kind of headaches that could make even the most seasoned entrepreneur break out in a cold sweat. Three thousand of three hundred thousand units arriving during the season we do 70 percent of our business—well, that's a recipe for disaster. Suddenly, our business is teetering on the edge, and we know something's gotta give.

So, what do we do? We pivot. We adapt. We roll up our sleeves and get down to business. And you know what? It's messy. It's chaotic. But it's also strangely exhilarating—like riding a roller coaster with no seat belts. We hustle, we grind, and have plenty of panic attacks. How can I let the last seventeen years go down the tubes and end after everything we fought for and conquered? Eventually, after a lot of conversations that sometimes made me want to vomit, we find a lifeline—a strategic partner with the firepower and muscle to help us weather the storm.

And just like that (I mean, not just like that, but because you don't have all day, I will keep those details for another time), we're in it for the long haul—a strategic investment, a new chapter, but the same ol' me at the helm. It's been three years now, and let me tell you, I've learned a thing or two along the way. Turns out, there are still no shortcuts to success. It's all about dedication, persistence, and a healthy dose of grit. Oh, and did I mention the importance of forming new relationships and navigating those murky waters with finesse?

Because let me tell you, integrating into a new company is no walk in the park. It's like entering a new relationship—exciting, nerve wracking, and full of surprises. But with a lot of communication, empathy, and patience, we're beginning to find our groove—both me and my team.

Now, here's the real kicker, the lesson I want you to take away from this wild ride:

Focus on making money and don't be scared to talk business with friends. I know that sometimes we just wanna show our kids' faces and talk about our sex lives or lack of it. But because we don't talk about money, because we don't share details of how we invest, spend, and accumulate wealth or move toward profitability, we as women are far behind. You know those golf outings that some husbands take? Guess what is being talked about: m-o-n-e-y. Yeah, yeah, I know—passion, purpose, all that jazz. But let's get real for a moment. If you're not turning a profit, you're just spinning your wheels on the business treadmill. Sure, it's fun for a while, but eventually, you're gonna burn out. And for another dose of reality, you won't just burn out, you might not grow, get investors, or be able to weather economic storms when they arise. Making a profit, putting aside funds for rainy days, and investing our money are how we will all have a more secure future and great economic impact.

In this new chapter, I want to share some of the strategies I've used to keep my personal cash flowing and the profits rolling in. It's all about saving for the future, investing in yourself, and building a business that can stand the test of time.

Because at the end of the day, that's what it's all about—building something that lasts. Something you can be proud of.

Here are a few of the helpful tips I wanted to share:

- **START A SAVINGS ACCOUNT.** I don't care if it's one with the lowest yield. Yup, that goes against anyone out there. Why do I say this? Well, because I just want you to start saving, no matter what or where. Heck, stash it in a lockbox in your house. Throw away the password, set it on auto, and let that money build. Of course, you should have a 401(k) and a savings account, but one of the best outcomes of a very messy former relationship was that he told me to open an account and forget it existed. Each year as I did better, I got ballsier setting money aside. And what do you know? When it came time to purchase a home, I was shocked at how much I had saved. And lest you think

I started with a big amount, nope, twenty dollars a week was all I had, and over the course of fifteen years, and adding more when I could, it grew and grew. So, you might not think you can put anything aside, but you can. And if you do, come thank me later.

- **INVEST IN WHOLE LIFE INSURANCE.** Now this isn't some sales pitch, and I am def not sponsored, but you will be *shocked* at the returns and tax-free income you get when you do this. Best part? It doesn't sink in value when the market does. I have no idea why this is such a hard-to-come-by secret. A fellow school mom is the one that told me about this, but had I known about this sooner, I would have done it and gone big. I now set aside money every year for this. To me, it's a hedge against the chaotic markets and something that has continued to pay over the last few years. Do your research. I am not a CPA or even close to a financial expert, nor should I be giving you the advice that a real professional gives. (But what the heck. It's what helped me, so sharing it with you here.)

- **OPEN UP YOUR OWN LLC AND PAY YOUR KIDS**, then watch the write-offs kick in. It's a sad day when you get your tax savings ideas from social media, but alas, here we are. I ran this up a few flagpoles, and lo and behold, today (2025) you can legally pay your kids up to $13,500 yearly, and they are not taxed and you get the write-off. Well, what are you paying them for? So many things! They are your social media models, they are your tiny assistants, helping you and your xyz.LLC thrive. Now you might be wondering, okay, so I paid them, now what! Well, let them build up credit by contributing to household purchases on a credit card, have them pay for school, or even open life insurance for them, and watch them become a millionaire or have college funds by the time they graduate. Every model I compared was more than any 401(k) or Roth, but you gotta start when they are young.

Now all this might sound overwhelming, and you might not even have the money to eat out. I hear ya. I was there, remember? But we all have to start, we all have to plan, and when you have anything extra, these would be my top places to spend it. I don't subscribe to the idea of don't-buy-your-matcha-and-save-instead. Buy your matcha if that makes you happy, or better yet, make it at home, and take all that extra money you saved by not getting it at the corner shop and put it aside. Watch it grow and reinvest.

It's time we get honest about money. It won't come from a tree, and it's up to us to go after it, make it, save it, and spend it.

I hope you enjoyed this book and bonus chapter, I hope it focuses things for you and that you get out there, attack life, and *win*.

Much love,
Rebecca

ACKNOWLEDGMENTS

I WANT TO DEDICATE this book to a shit ton of humans, so bear with me:

Mom: Thank you for being an ever-present inspiration—not for that newest, hottest nylon backpack you dream of me making, but for your way of getting me to learn on my own and fight for what I want, and for your belief that I could figure it out. I hope that Bowie learns these wonderful life lessons from you as she goes about her journey.

Dad: Thanks for saying no. Simply put, I have learned a lot from your resolve and determination to be great at what you do, despite the odds. You have been there for me through all my bad boyfriends, my failures, and my success, and I am grateful for your endless support.

Uri: It has been a fifteen-year ride. I would not have made it here without your ability to let this company have its nine lives. You have shown me that persistence, grit, and wit pay off in spades. Thanks for taking the call and being an incredible partner.

Max: To the brother who played Barbies with me, pulled me around in cardboard boxes, and humored me by wearing pants made backward and sideways. Your love and care for others is what has always made you so special.

Gavin: You shacked up with me when this was a dream. Thank you for your love and support and for being an incredible husband and friend. You're the best circus comanager I could have ever wished for.

Osman: Thank you for believing in this company and for going out on more than a limb to support and foster its success. You are our fairy godfather.

Michael and Peter: What a ride! Thank you for your endless patience, for floating us, for hanging on, and for your belief in us when you knew you should walk but you didn't. You are the best banking partners a business can ask for. I am endlessly grateful.

Jody: Almost fifteen years ago, you walked into a tiny apartment after I ran a classified, and you never looked back. Thanks for being such an incredible partner and leader and such a steadfastly loyal friend and colleague. I love ya.

Kenny: You have been a teacher and a wise man who has taught me more about life than I imagined. Thank you for taking a chance on me and for being there when the books said to run. You have a heart of gold.

Richard: You helped take a cute company and make it grow into what we are today. Your heart has been in this since day one, and while we have truly tried your sanity, you have been there for us over and over.

Craig: You are the ultimate block and tackle. You have made this mission yours. I am ever so grateful for your endless help and dedication and for you always being a source of laughter in this hectic business.

Jenna: You are truly my fairy godmother. Had you not taken a chance on my silly shirt and asked me to make a bag, I simply wouldn't be here. I am forever grateful.

To the ladies—Kumi, Cynthia, Jill, Elissa, Trang, Jen, Ilaria, Stephanie, Tamara, Robyn, Daniela, Tali, Kat, Eden, Elisabeth, Ali, Jenna A., Sam, Tara, and Elisha: You are all the reason I get to be here. I am so grateful for the support you've given me, for the push, and for the tough love, and that you've been my amazing support system throughout this crazy life in fashion.

Crystal: I would simply not be here if it were not for you. You put me on the map. You have supported this dream from day one, and I am endlessly grateful. We've come full circle. Thank you for helping bring these stories to life.

To my team: We don't get to achieve our dreams by doing things alone. It's a group effort, and anyone who has come through our doors has helped shape our company in some way and helped make this dream come true. Thank you!

Okay, okay, okay! I know that was a long one. Thanks for bearing with me. And thank YOU for being with me every step of the way.

ABOUT THE AUTHOR

REBECCA MINKOFF is a fashion designer and serial entrepreneur. She founded her namesake label in 2001 with a T-shirt
and, through its success, built the globally recognized accessible luxury brand for which she is known today. In 2018, she
tapped into the power of knowledge and community with
the launch of both her *Superwomen* podcast and the Female
Founder Collective to enable and empower women-led businesses across industries. Rebecca lives in Brooklyn with her
husband and three children. This is her first book.

NOW THAT YOU'VE HEARD my story and the rules that had to be broken, reinvented, and rewritten, it's time for you to chart your own path. Let's keep the conversation going. Join me and the other women who are breaking barriers every day. Scan this code for more content to help you on your own journey.